BLACK AMERICAN MUSIC:

Past and Present

by

Hildred Roach

CRESCENDO PUBLISHING CO.

BOSTON

ACKNOWLEDGMENTS

Outstanding among the many persons and organizations who deserve my sincere gratitude for their inspirations and contributions are: pioneers of Black Studies Margaret Wilson, Maud Hare, Benjamin Brawley, Alain Locke, John Work III, Margaret Butcher, Edgar Toppin, Langston Hughes, Lerone Bennett and John Franklin; composers Hale Smith, Ulysses Kay, John Carter, Noel DaCosta and others who supplied invaluable research information in addition to highlights of their own careers; publishers and consultants: Edward B. Marks, Oliver Daniel of Broadcast Music and J. K. Nketia of the University of Ghana; family, friends and colleagues Altona Johns, Dr. Vivian McBrier, Antoinette Handy-Miller, Geneva Southall, Maurice Strider, Robert Felder, Roger Askew, Nathaniel Williams, Mrs. John W. Work III, Percy Gregory, Mildred Ellis, Harvey and Florence Van Buren, William and Shirley Moore, Cheryl Moulton, Joseph Gathings, Jeanne McRae, Annie W. Roberts, Susie Graham, Adelaide P. Wicks and Attorney H. Carl Moultrie; librarian Ulysses Cameron; clerical assistants Raymond Jones, Carl Roach and Dianne Spann; photographers Scott and Merceron of Scurlock Studios; and Ruby Roach Satterwhite, who sketched instruments and planned rough designs associated with the text.

I am greatly indebted to Dr. Oscar Henry of Fisk University for his criticism and reading of the book in its earliest form, and to Ruth and Bernard Colner for their proofreading assistance. My thanks are also extended to Edward Owens, editor, and to Robert Bell of Crescendo Publishers for their patience and appraisals. My Mother, Pearl, constantly encouraged the completion of this project, and to her I give the highest praise of all: the dedication of this book.

HILDRED ROACH

Library of Congress Catalog Card Number: 72-87762

ISBN 0-87597-079-6

Printed in the United States of America

To my mother, Pearl

CONTENTS

ILLUSTRATIONS

PREFACE

The need to survey African-American composers and their music is real and immediate. This book is intended to meet this need and present a balanced view of the involvement of Blacks in various types of music. An interrelationship will be demonstrated between African musical sources and North American composers. Also, a logical conclusion is to show that some Black music influenced, and was influenced by, European music.

Since each facet of this music cannot be examined here, composers and musical forms are stressed rather than performers, the latter being discussed only where they serve to classify anonymous composer-performers of a significant era or style. This book covers aspects of Black music which are usually omitted from standard music history books. Therefore, it should supplement such established works. It is, then, a recall of Black developments to be placed alongside other proud assets of fellow Americans.

Black American Music: Past and Present may be used for courses in Black music or with books of introduction, listening or analysis of music. Teachers and students should find the contents helpful as a guide to composers and their music, and the general public may find it useful as source material to correlate with any field or specific knowledge. Hopefully, this work will promote a necessary identity among Blacks universally, as well as inform others of a proud and genuine heritage of these contributions not only in American music, but in American history.

The author suggests that the readers make full use of the materials found in the list of musical terms, the list of composers and publishers of the music discussed and the additional readings and recordings. All efforts must be made to promote the listening, performing and understanding of the music that is Afro-American.

PART ONE

THE BEGINNING (1619-1870's)

I
SLAVE ERA:
THE BLACK MAN IN COLONIAL AMERICA

The first generation of Black slaves in America were Africans. This slave trade together with the Civil War and Reconstruction served as the background for the earliest musical contributions by anonymous Blacks.

By the process of either bargaining or stealing, Africa became the prime source of American slaves. Although taken from various areas of the country, the greatest number of Africans were gathered from points nearest the Gulf of Guinea. One of the strongest and most famous of these West African areas was Ashanti (modern Ghana) whose magnificent coasts along Tema, Accra, Winneba, Cape Coast and Elmina became common ports of call. However, many parts of Africa remained untouched by European traders, and certain distant locations from the coast, such as Egypt, supplied only a small number of slaves, as the journey prevented large numbers from surviving the ordeal of the desert.

The original home of the Africans was considered backward and uncivilized by White Americans, and Blacks were made to believe this. However, Africa was a country of many languages, cultures and world foundations. Even within a small radius, thousands of tribal constituencies such as Ashanti, Wa, Twi, Akan, Ga, Ewe, Kwa, Yoruba, Mandingo, Tshi and Ibo evidenced this variety. This factor must have contributed to the difficulty in communicating not only with the slave traders, but with respective Africans as well. There were also several social, political and religious practices found among the African Christians, Moslems and Voodooists which further complicated the process of assimilation among Africans, and thus helped in the perpetuation of slavery itself.

However diverse, each tribe had some things in common. Individually, each had practiced a long history of social organization, politics, teaching, learning and general development. Each had boasted a populace of chieftains, architects, craftsmen, doctors, warriors, scientists and musicians and each had planned its own mores, religion, government and social commitments. Each was more geographically linked than modern politics now indicate.

Africans populated Abyssinia (Ethiopia) with its regal splendor and strong lineage; Egypt, with the spectacular pyramids; and Mali, which boasted not only Timbuktu as a famous center of learning, but its famous patron kings and court musicians. If we are to believe historians Herodotus and others, Africa also served as a spawning ground for related theories

3

fused into ancient western civilizations identified with Greece and Rome; these theories ironically built upon the best customs of those who eventually became subjects to the western world.

Had the Black man been taught the value of his heritage, he might have had a stronger ego, full of pride for himself and his brother, and an adequate regimen of satisfactions in the accomplishments of his people. He might have developed a love for the strength of his culture, his craftsmanship, and his music. However, he was forced to leave this heritage and begin anew in a world where his ideas of music and art were little known and yet to develop. Little did he know that his musical nature and spiritual stimuli would be so important in the development of the New World.

Since tribal roots and other cultural associations of Africa were eventually banned, the older heritage meant nothing to those whose majority of melodies sprang from beneath the level of human society. Having been reduced to rank and status of pigs and horses, they were termed "chattel." Denied the education common to Whites, African languages and structures were soon forgotten.

During slavery, mistreatment and deprivations which accompanied these conditions were constant. Although slavery had existed in Africa and other parts of the world wherein Whites had also been enslaved, nowhere did reports seem to outdo the mountain of wrongs enforced upon the Blacks as in America. But American slavery is not the real question here. The point of this discussion is to bring out these elements of society whose intense bitterness within oppression produced the multiplicity of passions that became the basis of Black music and to show the general conditions under which an art may grow. These elements must be considered for a valid understanding of some characteristics common to Black music.

In early 1619, Black slaves entered Virginia, according to Lerone Bennett. They were then transported to other parts of America (see maps). Slaves became concentrated in the southern states mainly because of the economic importance of cotton. And even though slaves were also maintained in northern states, they were not in great number. Therefore, the majority of the earliest musical endeavors emanated from the geographical areas of the South.

Slave narratives written by Frederick Douglass and Sojourner Truth show that because slave owners were suspicious and fearful of insurrections which had occurred both on ship and land, slaves were "forced" to sing their songs so that it could be assumed that they were not planning other incidents. Consequently, such music was often molded from inhuman experiences of slavery, and was used to forget the conditions under which they worked. Music also relieved the burden of their problems, both physical and spiritual, and at times, served as a signal to amuse themselves.

To sing and play were not new to the Africans, whose functional art was interwoven into their everyday life. Yet to perform under such conditions was an experience to which they were not accustomed. Nevertheless,

4

the strength of their character and their natural talents surfaced under circumstances that might have destroyed weaker men. They poured their emotions into the music that told that part of the American story which now provides a basis for the cultural awakening of Blacks in our time.

Early slave music consisted of many human passions derived from oppression. Spirituals, blues, hollers and work songs were some examples which echoed emotional despair as well as jubilation and optimistic yearning for a Utopia — a better place without a master, without auction blocks and without conditions of servitude. These songs, both simple and complicated, had grown out of the duties and the drudgery associated with bondage and had served for work, worship and play. Many such creative influences were vestiges of their own Africa.

No doubt, many of the earliest songs were sad. It is incorrect to assume, however, that all were of this nature, for within a span of some 200 years, slaves knew both sadness and happiness. Revealing the functional categories of African music, many songs collected during Reconstruction reflected individual and collective thoughts of diverse situations of life and emotion. For example, those Africans toiling under burdensome circumstances undoubtedly composed one way while those treated more humanely naturally composed another. Likewise, music used for funerals differed from that used for entertainment. Thus, slave texts referred to a gamut of emotions.

Even though commenting on only one musical form, Frederick Douglass, born and educated as a slave, was of the opinion that all spirituals seemed sad. In his autobiography, *My Bondage and My Freedom,* he wrote:

> I did not, when a slave, fully understand the deep meaning of those rude and apparently incoherent songs . . . . They breathed the prayer and complaint of soul overflowing with the bitterest anguish . . . . The remark . . . that slaves were the most contented and happy laborers in the world . . . was a mistake . . . to suppose . . . . The songs represented their sorrows, rather than their joys.
> Slaves were expected to sing as well as to work . . . [as] a means of telling the overseer, in the distance, where they were and what they were about . . . those commissioned to the Great House farm were peculiarly vocal . . . . While on the way they would make the grand old woods for miles around reverberate with their wild and plaintive notes. They were indeed both merry and sad. Child as I was, these wild songs greatly depressed my spirits.

Many have used his statements to assume that all slave songs were sad, without first considering that not all spirituals were sad. Nor were the countless other songs experienced within 200 years completely sad. For one thing, some Blacks had managed a share of the material goods before the Civil War and were pleased with their possessions. Others were either too young to comprehend the situation or were too happy to have escaped hopeless conditions of serfdom and indebtedness at home. Still others, like the Black cowboys or a very few nomads, were without many of the cares of southern slavery. In addition, many songs of joy arose from the Black

5

populace once Emancipation appeared imminent or when a slave successfully escaped.

It was not entirely the music, then, but the slavery itself which described the real sorrow that Douglass must have felt, and which penetrated the environment around which all such songs were created. Music was wrongly accused, for music had the power to induce boundless happiness. By soothing the souls and healing the sick, it could create an aesthetic quality of mind beyond recall. It could quench hate, develop a mock peace and pronounce a man "free" from the cares of slavery and Reconstruction.

All this was the power of the music composed by Blacks. For theirs was a practical art which lived as they lived. More important than the fact that the songs later served as historical data, is the realization that these songs directly functioned in the plans and survival of the Blacks from the era of Nat Turner to that of Martin Luther King. The strong characteristics and inbred qualities found in the African people and their songs prepared them for the coming transition in building a new way of life, their own language and a new music.

Fig. 1a. Guardian Figure Mask, West Africa.
Courtesy of Fisk University.

6

Fig. 1b (above). Elmina Castle, a slave fort in Ghana, West Africa.
Fig. 1c (below). Ganvie Sea Village, Cotonou, Dahomey.

II
AFRICAN HERITAGE:
AN INFLUENCE IN MUSICAL TRADITION

In order to define Black American music, we must first consider Africa as the source of the talents developed in compositions from the earliest to the present. For throughout slavery, the proofs of an African heritage were evident in the elements of early African-American music. As the slaves steadily produced successive generations of offspring, the influence of their African characteristics and those of Europe merged to create the modern era of Americanism. Consciously or subconsciously, Old Africa, the Mother Country of civilization, remained the most important source of originality for Blacks, and eventually for many musical attempts in American nationalism.

In order to further comprehend this African spirit within an artistic realm of Afro-American music, we must seriously study Africa in relation to its people and its culture. For example, one could recall the multi-tribal complexities which enhanced the African social systems. This fact alone assured that great varieties of musical substances would exist in early slave music. When compounded, these innumerable features defined the music as a distinctive collection of sounds marked by diverse improvisation in performance with melismatic or ornamental melodies, exciting dances, complex rhythms, unique harmonies, scales, forms, titles and textures.

The definition of African music represented the core of Black music in America. In Africa, the soul of music evolved from an inseparable combination of the sister arts of music with drama and dance, and became expertly woven into the language and customs of the people. These elements blended according to the event, appropriateness of the vernacular, age, sex and status of the participants. Yet neither instrument, form, peer group, text, dance, nor musical elements could be taken out of the context of the event for which the music was planned. Neither could any of these elements or media be mixed unless prescribed by tradition.

African instruments, costumes, accessories and dramatic reactions were dictated by the correlation of the composite arts of music, drama and dance and one would be meaningless without the other. Seen in various activities, this correlation weighed heavily on the importance of speech and life itself. For example, a dramatic play or story could include the spontaneous interpolation of music and dance and could be based on actual experiences such as hunting or harvesting. A master drummer would begin a pattern based on word derivatives, inspiring dancers to sing and to act out words with a life-like reality and emotion. A funeral would require appropriate costuming, instruments, textual references to the decedent's history, dirges, specific peer characters, appropriate prayers and dances. All of the above demonstrated necessary elements of cohesiveness.

African music generally involved a close relationship between performers and the community. For example, the funeral mentioned could begin with dirges and prayers from the family members, and gradually include members of the total community or village. Singers were answered by a communal response, a technique referred to as "call and response" which was later reflected in religious sermons, jazz and other forms of the Afro-American.

The method of oral tradition was greatly responsible for the maintenance of the samples of African heritage which miraculously survived the centuries. Because of the illiteracy of most Blacks (at least in the English language) and because of the diversity of African languages, a process of rote teaching was instrumental in sustaining the legends and music of old Africa. Although many Africans had composed their own symbols to represent language sounds, the oral tradition was still by far the most common practice in Africa for decades, and remained the most effective method of reaching the thousands of slaves in America.

Oral tradition must be held responsible for one of the most exciting aspects of African and Afro-American performance — that of improvisation, or improvised variation. When passed orally, music was subject to change in its generation, transportation, and reception. The ornamentation of melodic tones, song forms, and accompanying body movements involved spontaneity and change from singer to singer, verse to verse, and from locale to locale. In speaking of African music, A. M. Jones pointed to this identical characteristic of improvisation, as have Ware, Allen and Garrison in their transcriptions of *Slave Songs.* This practice of variation marked almost each performance and was often suggested at the will of the master drummer or the lead singer. It must be understood that, in African music, this freedom to vary the structure depended upon the basic underlying form and that only specific points within the pieces were used for addition or alterations. Melodic alteration, however, was more liberal, as is seen in Black American music.

Words, Rhythm and Dance

The most important factor of African music seems always to have been the text. African languages themselves were musical in the spoken dialogue and demanded that pitches be relatively perfect for correct communication. One notes a similarity between this and the "sing-song" speech of southern Blacks. Even drum idioms attempted high and low imitations of speech intonations when they were performed on female and male instruments whose small and large sizes denoted levels of pitch sounds. Therefore, the "talking drums" were capable of sending out vital messages which were clearly understood by the population. So important were the words

9

that they served as the basis around which were formulated the remaining musical elements of melody, harmony, rhythm, form and timbre. According to J. K. Nketia, Professor at the University of Ghana, the words could be realized by modern musical transcriptions as in Example 1, and could suggest to a composer the actual elements of music.

Ex. 1. A representation of textual influence in African music.

Text   "Wo ho te sen?" (How do you do?)

Tone levels   low high, low high

Rhythm   short long, short long

Melody

Because of its impact upon the total American population, rhythm, or movement, was considered a most basic characteristic of African music, and essentially made it unique from any other forms. Much like the principle used in liturgical chants of western music, rhythm was dictated by the flow of words and generally reflected African life styles. From the city markets to the countryside villages, rhythm imitated the movements of the various lingual and human activities, whether fast or slow. When transcribed into western terminology, traditional African compositions showed life's constancy and tribal diversities through both complex and simple rhythms of time, space, energy and change.

Although duple and triple rhythms could be detected, actual beats within transcribed measures were not restricted to strong or weak beats, as in western music, but rather to word emphasis. Nor were the measures always in even numbers of four, eight or sixteen. While not composed in the same symmetry of design, this employed a freedom of "over the bar phrases" as felt in the music of J. S. Bach, or even a feeling of nonmeasure. Thus the odd numbers of measures were balanced by a more correct representation with emphasis on speech. These resulting designs of three, five or seven measures, while common to contemporary music, were nevertheless somewhat strange to the ears of the early Euro-Americans.

Because of the complexities of simultaneous rhythms or poly-rhythms, the overall metric patterns showed changes within sections, or denoted measures which could be interpreted as either three or six beats, or as two triplet beats. That is, a 3/4 meter could sometimes be interpreted as 6/8, and 6/8 could easily be felt as 2/4. Often during the course of a piece, such metric obscurity would smoothly shift from duple to triple time, as in Example 2. Since music was generally of the oral tradition, the metric complexities were not compositionally planned for the manuscript in western

10

terms. However, modern transcriptions of traditionalism do indicate such findings.

Ex. 2.   Polyrhythm and metric combinations in obscurity.

Another composition collected by A. M. Jones for his second volume of *Studies in African Music*, the *Agbadza*, a social dance, reveals more combinations of sounds which travel in polyrhythms scored for seven parts. In addition to the instruments represented on the printed score, it is also noted that accompanying rhythms from dancers would also become a part of the already complicated transcription seen in Example 3 (page 12).

In general, rhythm patterns ♪♪ or ♪♪ were favored. Many of these rhythmic idioms were found within compositions of the New World, from spirituals and hollers to jazz. The following chart of rhythms shows traditional African patterns which were inherited by the Afro-Americans. Taken from melodies transcribed from African sources, it shows multi-meters, delays, prolongations, offbeats or additives, triplets and smaller beats.

Ex. 4.   Chart of African rhythms.

Triplets				
(Additives) Syncopation				
Offbeat & Rhythmic Delays				
Multi-meters				
Prolongation				

Words and rhythms were copied by the human body in the dances which almost invariably accompanied the music. Through the medium of dance, Africa spoke in intricate movements of joys and sorrows, religion, love, abandonments and war. Among other events, dance was used at celebrations, recreations, marriages, youth rituals, worship and funerals. When used in worship, dance was not considered sacrilegious, but only as worshipful as the 150th Psalm which encouraged one to "Praise Him with timbrel and dance." When otherwise used, dance was as natural an accompaniment to the songs as were the overpowering drums.

In America, dance also occurred at various events, both secular and sacred. Afro-Americans inherited African features of ornamentation or variation upon the basic language of all dance — from complex improvising in walking, running and jumping, to formations of circular, linear or spiraling movements. One dance, the religious shout, was similar to the

11

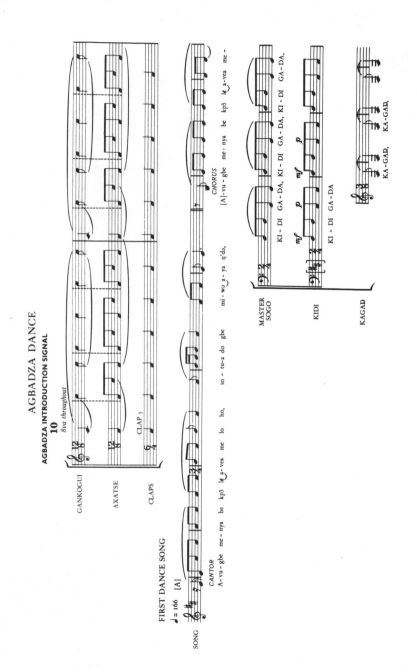

Ex. 3. *Agbadza Dance* (Social Dance), from *Studies in African Music* (Vol. 2), by A. M. Jones (Oxford University Press). Used by permission.

frenzied dances of fetish chiefs or warriors and was evidently used at both religious and secular outings. The ring games of children and later, the popular dances of the stage also included many effects which were inherited from African recreation. Still others of African background included the calinda, habenera rhythms, mabunda and various voodoo derivatives along with the bamboula, a hybrid version of which is shown in Example 5.

Ex. 5. *The Bamboula*

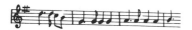

Melody and Harmony

Melody was suggested by the rise and fall of vocal inflections. When polylinear tones (many melodies) were combined in African music, the resulting combination became harmony. Melody and harmony were both planned by tribal practices which varied from a mixture of Asian and African elements in the Eastern region to strict African ornamentations in the West. Quite frequently African harmony appeared to grow melodically, either as overlapping melodies, or as melodic calls with harmonic answers. The latter technique was simulated in early Afro-American spirituals and hollers, etc.

An important feature of African melody was its constant change and variation, or ornamentation. Similar to western characteristics of vocal religious chants from the middle ages, vowels were extended over several different notes, complete with pitch waverings resembling trills or vibrato. These vowels involved quarter tones, which are somewhat smaller than half steps, and much like the Asian scale which is constructed on the sitar. Other ornaments also common to African melodies were the glissando, slides and grace notes. Not only were the melismatic melodies under constant ornamentation, but modern transcriptions show variations in actual repeats of verses or refrains.

Further melodic analysis suggested common harmonies and depending on local practice, African melodies made use of many scales, intervals and other combinations which westerners call modal. Each scale often had varieties of tone patterns which could lend themselves to either diatonic, chromatic or quarter tone movements. Simple harmonic accompaniments sometimes used thirds, fourths and fifths, but were usually conceived as polymelodies. In his *Studies in African Music,* A. M. Jones has demonstrated these points by the use of scientific diagrams depicting melodic and speech patterns of various locales.

Even though some African elements were also common to periods of western music, the total performance indicated a difference between European music and early Afro-American music. This was particularly true of both the ornamental variation in Black performances, the characteristic accompaniments and the overall manner of presentation. The following

13

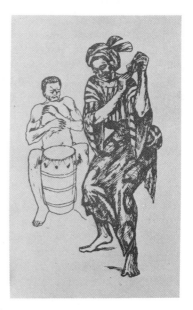

Fig. 2a (above). Young girls from Fanti village await signal to dance. Fig. 2b (right). Dancer receives cue from master drummer.

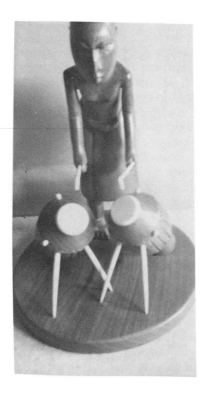

Fig. 3a (left). Wooden figure playing pair of spider (atumpan) drums. Fig. 3b (above). Percussion instruments (left to right): single bell, talking drums (bommaa), double bell, apentemma drum.

Example 6 represents some features listed above which continued during the early American days.

Ex. 6.   Melodic and harmonic characteristics of African music

     a. Ornaments: trill, slide and grace note.
     b. Scales: a heptatonic, hexatonic and pentatonic type.
     c. Intervals and harmonies.

Western concepts of harmonic progressions and strict rules of tonal centers were not evident in African music, although they later became adopted by African-Americans. The duration of notes was also not as strict, as in western cadential or sectional endings. Songs could terminate on long or short notes such as the eighth or sixteenth, and harmonies could step or skip about in parallel movements of sixths. Consonances generally characterized the overall harmonic strength, as shown above. If West African music approached the idea of a standard cadence, it was through the frequent use of the downward interval of a third (Example 6c), a characteristic feature also seen in terminating phrases in Afro-American blues.

Form

The form or structure of African compositions represented the end product of improvised or planned music. Its shape contained an overview of harmony, melody and rhythm. Form was also dependent upon the text around which it was constructed. By its title, form implied the media for performance, such as the instrumentation, sex and approximate age group. In general, these forms were represented at incidental, occasional or recreational events. Into the first group went songs for work, games, storytelling and the like. Occasional music included that usually reserved for the royal houses, for festivals, special groups and ceremonies. Recreational music implied music used in groups for both young and old and centered around events.

——Some African songs were complex in organization and performance, sometimes involving a return to the beginning of the song as in the western "dal segno," or of alternating at intervals between one, two or three lead singers and chorus. Binary form was used, and this two-part structure also influenced Afro-American blues. Variations and suites were common as were verses with refrain, or strophic form, being spontaneously composed according to the whims of the lead singers. Whatever the form, dancers, instrumentalists and singers were all limited by the lingual framework, as suggested in the formal examples given below.

15

Adowa:	Music and dance for mixed group; suite of eight movements, with order depending upon direction of master drummer. Used for funeral or band music; sometimes with short sections and closing refrain.
Kundum:	Series of warrior dances forming a suite; expressed spirit and sentiments of Nzema and Ahanta people during festivals; showed bravery, thanks for harvest, prowess and endurance.
Akom:	Suite of dances performed by fetish priests which served to bring the priest out of a trance; contained both secular and religious elements.
Fontonfrom:	Series of warrior dances forming a suite; motions symbolic of combat; 77 proverbs uttered on drum and followed by dancer.
Nnwonkoro:	Intended for women, mainly adults; this form was sung for entertainment; having various themes of loved ones, one or two cantors alternated with chorus, clapping and swinging in place.

Timbre

The characteristic sound peculiar to any instrument or voice is its timbre. African instruments which included winds, strings and percussion, were handmade of materials at hand. A drum constructed from a membrane gave a dull or low timbre when relaxed, or a sharp, exciting clash when tightened. The voice could be nasal or throaty, depending upon the choice of the locale, and much like the blues singers in America, could not be justly appraised by western standards of singing, or even by groups from another African locale. Also dictated by taste, African timbres were further expanded by additions of spider webs, tassles, jingles, paper and other objects which, when attached to instruments, were capable of enhancing their tone qualities.

Egyptian art and Biblical psalm texts revealed a great deal about types of instruments used in ancient Africa. African instrumentation, according to historians Curt Sachs, Donald Grout and Robert Stevenson, provided much of the background for western timbres developed in ancient Greece and Rome, as well as in Asia. African history also points to the fact of distant travels by kings and court musicians, or griots, who were responsible for some of the exchanges and influences of musical ideas long before the middle ages and early Biblical references.

Some instruments seen in Africa today are the same types as those described in documents written by explorers centuries ago, well before the ominous year of 1619. Traditionally, these instruments were carefully sculptured and reflected grace, beauty, intricacy of design and practicality. This craft was carefully or sometimes crudely copied in America by Africans who remembered the original, and who produced products from the gutbucket, bones and gourds to the banjo.

In America, instruments from Europe were delivered which bore marks of greater refinements in construction. These mingled in pleasant interchanges with their counterparts of African ancestry. Around the fifteenth century, Africans had earlier bargained with peaceful European explorers for western-made violins. They encountered the violin in

16

America some decades later and continued using it. Some of the African products which had influenced the history of instruments are listed below:

Winds:	Flutes (single and double reeds); wia, chivoti, auleru, odurogya. Trumpets and horns (shells, calabash, ivory, wood, elephant tusks); Makondere, magwala, nyele, hieni, ntahera, awe.
Strings:	Harp, lyre, lute, zither: Tongoli, ndongo, kundi, ko, kora, ntongoli, litungu, thum, ekakira, kono, gonje, ligombo, tobo.
Percussion:	Drums, bells, gongs, jingles, xylophone: gourds, atumpan, atsimevu, donno, apentemma, kidi, nnawuta, frikyiwa, adenkum, ntara, kende, ngelenge.

Because of their great variety, and their dominant positions within the musical practices of Africa, drums were decidedly most important. In imitation of the percussive throb of the human body, drums characterized the rhythmic flow of the strength which must have accompanied the original Africans to America (see Fig. 3).

Texture

As seen earlier, melodic and homophonic elements together with poly-melodies and polyrhythms were generally common and could be produced by the following: a melodic sound of a leader, or two lead singers, followed by the vertical sounds of a chorus. The chorus could also produce polyphony or countermelodies, rather than homophony. Varieties of this music overlapped to make imitation possible within the polyphonic examples.

One overlapping texture was termed "hocket" by musicologists of the modern era. Performed on instruments possessing a limited range, the tones required to sound a piece were shared among several instruments which took turns playing at the proper time. Generally, the notched flutes with approximately three notes each would perform such melodies together, or other instruments would develop a total composition by the same process. Although involving time and precision, "hocket" as used here did not refer to the rhythmic principle of western music in the middle ages. Texture was made up of timbre, melody, harmony and rhythm, and denoted the total product of these elements.

Well versed in songs for every occasion, African tribes had used music as a practical art which reflected all facets of everyday living. Each tribe had insisted ·that its members enjoy the art of music-making. Having learned it at infancy and having retained the love of this music, many Africans were accomplished musicians upon arrival in America. It is correct to conclude that this tradition as practiced by Africans was passed on to the early Afro-Americans. To the Afro-Americans, the idea of functional music was real. The varieties of compositional techniques were utilized in the early slave songs and in more recent forms. Many composers became true pioneers in their love for this new music and reinforced the tradition of their forefathers.

17

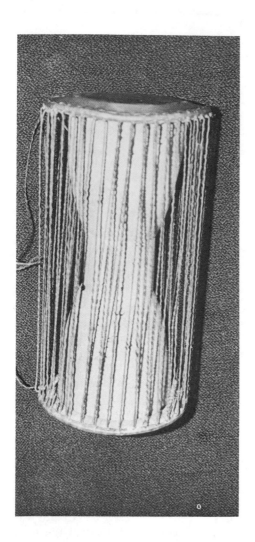

Fig. 4a (left). Donno drum with stick. Pressure or hourglass drum is placed under arm and is squeezed to make high and low pitches. Fig. 4b (above). Stringed instrument with gourd amplifier, sometimes played by plucking while partly resting in the mouth (musical bow).

Fig. 4c (above). Beaded gourd, usually shaken by women. Fig. 4d (below). Stringed instrument: gonje with bow.

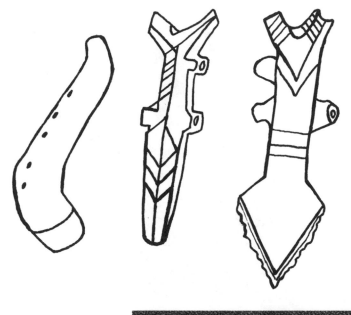

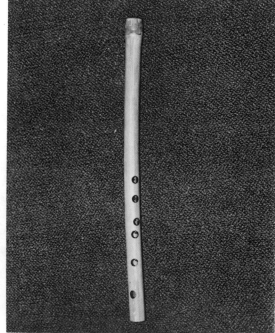

Fig. 4e (above). Wind instruments: ivory horn, two notched wooden flutes (wia). Fig. 4f (right). Wind instrument: bamboo flute.

III
EARLY FOLK MUSIC

Early folk music flourished from the time of the Baroque and Classical periods of western music to the era of the Romantic period, spanning the lives of the European composers from Frescobaldi to George Bridgetower, Coleridge-Taylor and Chopin. During the first agonizing days, the multi-functional music was more African than American, gradually transforming itself into Afro-American sacred and secular forms.

Inspired by the same environmental roots and conditions, secular songs grew alongside religious songs with an interrelationship that was often indistinguishable. That is, the subject of a call or holler could well be addressed to the same God of the spirituals discussed in Chapter four. This uniqueness was caused by the fact that, unlike African traditionalism which restricted its music to appropriate functions and events, slaves were not allowed to freely participate in all aspects of life common to African customs. Consequently, worship, work and relaxation were often performed under identical surroundings. Because of this unfortunate arrangement, neither could the strict definition nor the traditional practice of African music in correlation with other arts always be maintained. Thus, many elements of dance, instrumentation and other responses were necessarily abandoned in America.

Nevertheless, early folk songs occasionally consisted of instrumental, dance and vocal music, despite the fact that modern transcriptions were not able to capture many authentic accompaniments. Yet since the majority of Africans were generally commanded to work at a rapid pace, it is possible that much of the music was vocal, or was vocal with percussive sounds of working tools. Unless the slaves were regularly hired out to other plantations as professional performers, the Black population was generally restricted to these vocal developments. To sponsor the serious study of a western instrument for a Black person was rare, although this was certainly the case in a few instances since posters announcing runaway slaves indicated that they might try to pass themselves off as free orchestra players, and since some others such as Elizabeth Greenfield did indeed excel as concert artists.

Calls, Cries, Hollers and Shouts

The earliest of songs — the field or street calls, cries, hollers, shouts, work songs and play songs — were among those virtually spontaneous examples whose charm and naivety of materials served as foundations for both innocent and complex organizations for successive decades. According to Webster, a "call" was defined as a "loud tone, a shout, an announcement, summon or signal." This definition was exactly the way in which the call was used during slavery; that is, a high-pitched or subdued yell or chant to somewhere or somebody, for the purpose of commanding attention or emoting individual expressions of relief, abandonment or sorrow. Sometimes relaxing, complaining, or sometimes ostentatious show-offs resembling an auctioneer or square dance caller, the tunes were used for various functions from expressing love to shouting out directions to fellow workers.

Calls were sometimes used interchangeably with other forms. Harold Courlander, in his *Songs From Alabama*, listed titles of *Hey Rufus, Father's Field Call, Children's Field Call, Woh Hoo* and others, while B. A. Botkin recorded *Mississippi Sounding Call, Unloading Rails, Tamping Ties* and *Heaving the Lead Line.* Even blues collected by Alan and John Lomax, Lewis Jones and John Work revealed editions of camp hollers which related directly to the call. The titles of calls, hollers and cries therefore represented similarities in function, but not necessarily in general structural make-up.

The "cry" was equivalent to either a wail as in pain, anger, religion, fright or sorrow. When used in the street for selling wares, it was simply a synonym for "call." The verses, however, generally were clever gimmicks commanding attention to the announcement. To holler was also to yell or shout, as in a call. Whites often referred to those slaves "hollering in the fields." Although a synonymous relationship was seen in the like definitions, the terms could also imply dynamics of expression such as a more frantic sound for the holler, versus the lower subtlety of a cry. Some cries collected by Arna Bontemps and Langston Hughes showed poems similar to those used in minstrelsy as *Watermelon Vendor's Cry, Waffle Man's Cry, Oyster Man's Cry, Six Negro Market Songs of Harlem* and *Street Chef.*

Strangely enough, "shout" also implied a loud voice as in a yell or call. But more importantly, it referred to a frenzied, trance like dance of spiritual joy. Inherited from African religious dances, these physical reactions to the word of God and salvation were accompanied by verbal whoops of joy, and were performed seriously or whimsically, both inside and outside of Protestant churches. Dances other than the shout were discussed in Chapter two and were further reflected in the paintings of James Cloney and William Sidney Mount.

Work and Play Songs

Work and play songs were action pieces which required body movements. Lyrics of work songs dealt with railroad building, wood chopping, hauling bales, and pulling barges, while play songs dealt with counting games, hiding, riding and other dramatic play. More so than field hollers, the messages of the work songs were accompanied by the rhythmic swing-

22

ing of a hammer as in *Steel Laying Holler, Rock Island Line* or *I've Been Working on the Railroad.*

—— Play songs, on the other hand, were lighter pieces inspired by comedy and cheerful recreation rather than drudgery and toil. Consequently, being less restrictive allowed for running in circles, stooping, rising and imaginary flying as suggested in the lyrics of *Little Sallie Walker,* or in zigzag motions as in *All Hid. Little Sallie Walker,* one of the most familiar of the play songs (see example 7), was sung by a ring of players encircling a single person who acted out the words of the song, and who finally chose his successor by a properly directed "shake":

Little Sallie Walker,   (A music)
Sittin' in the saucer.
Rise, Sallie, rise, and
Wipe ya' weeping eyes, and
Fly to the east, and
Fly to the west, and
Fly to the very one that you love the best! (B music)

Chorus
Put'cha han' on ya' hip and
Let'cha backbone slip!
Shake it to the east, and
Shake it to the west, and
Shake it to the very one that you love the best!

It is significant to note that with the exception of the play songs, all of the early folk forms discussed here were associated with work. Even though it is true that calls, cries and hollers contained many different kinds of lyrics, their main purpose was to sustain one during his labor and to assist in selling or issuing directions. For the Blacks, the emphasis in early American life was placed on work, not play. Nevertheless, the origins of these songs did not preclude the fact that some were later used in minstrel performances as clever comic tunes or as stump recitations.

Text and Technique

Originally, work pieces consisted of actual African texts or lyrics with music, not necessarily in rhyme. Later, slaves set European dialect to African music, or vice versa, much like the two examples below which were taken from Arna Bontemps' and Langston Hughes' *The Book of Negro Folklore,* entitled *Cala Vendor's Cry* and *Street Chef:*

Tout chaud [all hot] madame,
Git 'em while they're hot! Hot Calas! (*Cry*)

Ah'm a natu'al bo'n cook
An' dat aint no lie,
Ah can fry po'k chops
An' habe a lo-down pie . . . .   (*Chef*)

From Saxon's *Gumbo Ya Ya.* Copyright, Houghton Mifflin Company. Used by permission.

23

The text of play songs showed the abandonment and carefree attitude of children at play. Sung in upward and downward intervals of thirds, or partly intoned in approximate pitches, *All Hid* was an example:

Five, ten, fifteen, twenty,
Twenty-five, thirty, thirty-five, forty,
Forty-five, fifty, fifty-five, sixty . . . . (*etc.*)
All Hid? (Ready or not, here I come!)

Textual phrases were sometimes half sung, half spoken or moaned. They became vocal techniques of syllabic, sporadic or ornamental styles which were passed on from composition to composition and were found in blues and spirituals as well as in many modern-day styles. In addition to the conventional poetry above, other sounds, both African and European were used, including prolongations of "ah," "oo," "ummm," "ee," "heh," "Lordy," "oh," "Jesus," "woh hoo," and "yeh." A single word could form an entire song through such elongations, or words could be interpolated between lines of other poetic structures to indicate an emotion or to ornament the music.

Characterized by short, sporadic, or long melodic lines, the forms and styles of these compositions ranged from simple to highly ornamental techniques. Variation, stanza without refrain and binary were common to the structures. According to present-day transcriptions, slides, grace notes, chromatics and ranges from seconds to sixths were plentiful, although occasional octaves and other intervals were also used. If most transcriptions of these were correct, they represented more complex ornamentations than were shown in the spirituals of that period. Yet modern transcriptions could not always denote actual performances since these compositions were both changed constantly and difficult to score. Just as in African music, cadences were not strict and pieces could terminate on any note of the scale. Example 7 shows some of these features along with some of the short forms which were common in early America.

Ex 7. Techniques and forms of early folk music. *Juba.* Reprinted by permission of Harvard University Press from *On the Trail of Negro Folk - Songs* by Dorothy Scarborough. Copyright 1925 by Harvard University Press; 1953 by Mary McDaniel Parker.

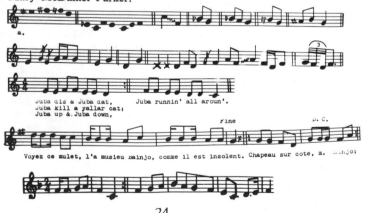

24

a. Chromatics, modes, word prolongation.

b. Slide, thirds, ornamentation and approximations; cadences.

c. Ballads: *Juba* (Reprinted by permission of Harvard University Press from *On The Trail Of Negro Folk-Songs* by Dorothy Scarborough, Copyright 1925 by Harvard University Press; 1953 by Mary McDaniel Parker); *Musieu Bainjo* from *Slave Songs* by Allen, Garrison and Ware and play song, *Little Sallie Walker* (traditional).

Like the spirituals and blues which they greatly influenced, these basic songs were usually in duple meter. This was true of street cries, work songs and play songs. However, many were also of free style rhythms emphasizing words or syllables. The connection of these small, unsophisticated forms cannot be discounted in the continual quest for a definition of Afro-American music, its origin, performance, history and technical styles.

IV
SPIRITUALS

Having been born somewhere between African voyages of the 1600's and American Reconstruction, spirituals were the end products of calls and hollers developed during early colonialism. Their exact origin cannot be established. Yet these anonymous songs have continually served as sources of inspiration for Blacks in their urgent quest for identity, heritage and a homeland.

Variously called jubilee, minstrel, religious, slave or folk songs, spirituals covered a wide range of subjects both religious and secular. They fell into a broad, all-inclusive definition as recorded in Webster's Dictionary: "of the spirit or the soul, often in a religious or moral aspect, as distinguished from the body; . . . concerned with intellect . . . showing much refinement of thought and feeling; spiritualistic or supernatural; a spiritual thing or concern . . ."

The words "often of a religious or moral aspect" generally did represent the feeling of the songs, but "often" did not imply "always." Despite the overabundance of Biblical words used in the majority of songs called spirituals, their functions were not purely religious. They were constantly used in the search of freedom, in religious services, to teach, gossip, scold, signal, or to delight in the telling of tales. Like work songs, calls and hollers, spirituals developed simultaneously in appeasement of the curiosity of the overseers who required a knowledge of the whereabouts or location of slaves. They also relieved the minds and bodies of the enslaved and they served more significantly as a practical means of informing the slaves of their own affairs, i.e., social politics, deliverance, escape or satire. As Webster has defined, the spirituals were also "concerned with the intellect" and were most refined in both "thought and feeling."

H. T. Burleigh called the spirituals the "spontaneous outbursts of intense religious fervor which had their origin chiefly in camp meetings, revivals and other religious exercises." Others have also conceded that spirituals resulted from the "introductions" of Christianity to slaves in America — a tactic intended to maintain docility among chattel.

While Christianity was perhaps instrumental in the use of a large number of words, it seems dogmatic to assume this in each case. In fact, not every such song preserved contained the elements of religion, nor was each used for only one purpose. There was much more ambiguity in designs, origins and functions than has generally been assumed. For

26

example, *Who Dat Comin' Over Yonder?*, *Git on Board, Little Chillen'*, *I Know de Udder Worl' Is not Like Dis*, *Die in de Fiel*, and *Same Train* (below) may or may not have been composed with any religious spiritualism in mind.

Same train, same train, same train carry my mother, [sister]
Same train, same train, same train carry my mother,
Same train be back tommorrer, same train, same train.

Same train a-blowin' at de station, same train, same train,
Same train a-blowin' at de station,
Same train be back tommorrer, same train, same train.

Christian kingdoms existed in Africa much earlier than slavery in America. However, some Africans were nevertheless introduced to Christianity by American colonists. Even though it is difficult to state their exact influence, it is safe to say that the collective experiences of both Africa and America served to produce the spirituals, and that the centuries of American mixtures resulted in the refined products as sung by the Fisk Jubilee Singers at Reconstruction.

Early collections of Black music contained more spirituals than other small forms. This indicated an importance attached to these songs. The earliest of these collections were compiled by Whites. In 1867, W. F. Allen, Charles Ware and Lucy M. Garrison published a collection entitled *Slave Songs in the United States,* and because of the geographic source of the islands off the coast of Georgia and South Carolina, their transcriptions were considered more traditional in dialect and performance than others collected within the city. Since that time, collections by Black composers James Weldon and J. Rosamond Johnson, John W. Work III, H. T. Burleigh, Hall Johnson, Nathaniel Dett and many more have followed.

Understandably, none of these could denote the exact dates of the compositions. Although such songs as *No More Auction Block for Me* must well suggest the era of Emancipation, this could be speculative reasoning as the origin of the song could also border on implications of death, love conditions or social solidification against slavery. Consequently, the best solution as to the dates of composition were those by W. E. B. DuBois and Benjamin Brawley who, in their books, *The Souls of Black Folk* and *The Negro Genius,* pointed out general periods of the following songs:

Early Period: *See Fo' and Twenty Elders on Deir Knees; You May Bury Me in de East; Nobody Knows; Swing Low, Sweet Chariot*

Middle Period: *March On; Steal Away; Bright Sparkles; I've Been A-Listenin' All de Night Long*

Late Period: *(Bright Sparkles); Dust, Dust and Ashes, My Mother Took Her Flight; I Hope My Mother Will Be There in That Beautiful World on High.*

27

Content and Purpose

Spirituals covered the history, thoughts and treatment of the Black Man. They pondered his fate, his everyday life, emotions and freedom. If some of the African-American history resembles that of the Jewish people, it was because of two main factors. First, Biblical events pinpointed Egypt as the site where the Jews were held in captivity and Ethiopia as the place where the Black Queen of Sheba gave birth to Solomon's son. The facts were therefore real to history. Second, if we are to believe the records of West African explorers from Europe, the captivity of Blacks, some of whom were Egyptians, caused them to assume a natural kinship. Where once the captors of the Jews had been their enemy, they now had become as brothers. Part of this history was unwittingly related in a folktale version of *Joshua Fit de Battle* or *When Israel Was in Egypt Land*:

Ex. 8. *When Israel Was in Egypt Land.* Traditional.

When Israel was in Egypt Land, Let My People Go,
Oppressed so hard they could not stand, Let my people go;
Go down, Moses, way down in Egypt land,
Tell ole Pharaoh, Let my people go.

Because they functioned as practical tools for emotional and physical escape, multifold purposes were assigned to the spirituals from religious expression to communication (by code). Many topics therefore reflected the diverse purposes and concerns of this era. From a hymn-style comment of *There's a Man Goin' 'Round Takin' Names* to an oral folktale version of *Old Noah, He Built Himself an Ark,* the spirituals were composed with allegorical or supernatural flavor, with deep expressions of mystical and religious emotions, or as with the gossip-like quality of *The Hypocrite and the Concubine*.

A. M. Jones states that African songs were "full of allusions and hidden meanings" and could not be translated without the help of an African, despite a knowledge of African words in definition. Even play songs or fishing songs could speak of a tale other than that understood by the words alone, without benefit of the interpreted message. If we accept the possibility that at least some of the spirituals retained an African heritage, then it would be easier to conclude that the following songs possibly contained various symbolic interpretations and connotations: *Steal Away; Good News, Member, I Heard From Heaven Today; Wade in de Water; You Go, I'll Go With You; I'll Meet You at the Station When the Train Comes Along* and *Ain't I Glad I Got Out of the Wilderness*.

Spirituals were further laden with obsessions about "freedom land", "home," utopias, "Jesus," "deliverer," or "Saviour." Some ambiguity or dual meaning could have pointed to "Jesus" or "Savior" as either the God of Christianity, Ntoa, the supernatural spirits of ancestors, or to a Harriet

28

Tubman of the Underground Railroad. Canaan may have depicted a Heaven, a better life to the north, or freedom after Emancipation. "Home" could have meant either Heaven or Africa. In any case, the slaves were eventually forced to resort to the use of words and actions of a significance contrary to that outwardly spoken or suggested. This fact alone implied a sound knowledge of English and prearranged communications among the slaves.

Melody and Harmony

Spirituals were sung in major, minor, modal or mixtures of scales. While a great majority could be analyzed within a major mode, they could also include both minor or modal scales simultaneously. Some already harmonized with western harmonies in modern transcriptions could be explained within scales common to Africa as well. For example, DuBois pointed to *Nobody Knows de Trouble I've Seen* and *Steal Away* as examples from the early period. Even though they both blended well with the major transcriptions, it was a fact that specific tones of the major scale were omitted in the original melodies, thereby generally reflecting the pentatonic scales:

Ex. 9. *Nobody Knows, Steal Away,* scale outlines. Traditional.

Some melodies of both the western and African systems agreed upon the predominant use of thirds, fifths and octaves. Consequently, the Afro-American examples fell into the same aural confines. Whereas African melodies of various tribes used thirds, fourths, sevenths and octaves as harmonies, the spirituals did not regularly employ many large skips in the linear or melodic intervals, but were more vocally diatonic and highly ornamented.

Some keys and chords were clearly outlined and confirmed by the melodies used, and others were not. For example, *Steal Away* and *Nobody Knows* implied a tonic chord at the beginning and ending. The following Example implies both tonic and dominant seventh chords in its melodic line.

Ex. 10. *Rock O' My Soul.* Traditional.

Rock O' My Soul in the bosom of Abraham; (Three times)
O Rock o' my soul!

Although the chords were not as problematic to western analysis as were the keys because of the agreement of consonances, keys remained a mystery for some time. In western music, most keys could be determined by cadential endings, though some have ended on the dominant or simply in another key from that found at the beginning. In African music, pieces could end on almost any note of the scale. As already discovered by Maud Hare, John Work and others, some spirituals used African concepts in arrangements of melodic tones, but generally concluded with western cadential patterns.

Melodic endings in songs of work, play or blues moved up or down a third toward a tonal center. Common endings in spirituals descended scalewise from three to one. Certain others ended a fourth, a second, or third below, or from a third above, as in Example 11. These melodic outlines could easily be harmonized using I, IV, and V, the customary chordal basis for confirming tonal centers in western music. Such harmonies were indeed eventually adopted by the Blacks who later assimilated things American.

Ex. 11.   Melodic techniques of spirituals.

a. Endings
b. Melodic ranges: *No Man Can Hinder Me; Just Been to the Fountain.*

According to documents by Ware, Allen, Garrison and others, the use of parts was spontaneous, and as there were no set rules, would occur at any given time during the performances. Examples ranged from several voices to a lead singer in alternation with other voices. Sometimes the solo voice was used as an improvised upper melody (obligato) over a chorus of harmony.

In general, frequent usage of consonances could be sustained by the common chords of the period (I, IV, V). These were in keeping with the broader, theoretical practices found in both folk and art music inherited from Europe. Even though the bass outlines (lowest overall melody) were not always sung as in western practices, most of the spirituals transcribed from live performances during Reconstruction showed strict use of these common chords. No doubt, as in some African music, many chords of the sixth were employed (having the third as the lowest tone of a chord) as well as original harmonies. However, these chords without roots as lowest tones were probably derived more from intervals than from any key concept at the beginning, and only later adapting to the customary key nomenclature of western music.

African melodies and scales had used a variety of tones which were changed by lowering and raising tones one-half step, or even a quarter tone. This was not a change in the scale, but simply a variation from one manner of rendering tones "straight." For that reason, a heptatonic scale (altered) could make use of the lowered sixth, seventh, or third. This idiom has consistently lasted in the spirituals, and has further influenced the history of jazz and other Black music. Although these features of jazz scales will be discussed at a later time, it is yet interesting to note that those

30

scales of the spirituals discussed by African scholars and those shown in David Baker's and John Mehegan's jazz studies are quite similar in concept. Some of these melodic variants brought from Africa were preserved in the spirituals shown in Example 12.

Ex. 12. *Come Go With Me* (transposed) and *The Hypocrite and the Concubine,* from *Slave Songs,* Allen, Garrison and Ware.

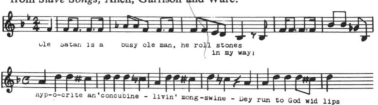

Ole Satan is a busy ole man, he roll stones in my way;

Hyp-o-crite an'concubine - livin' mong-swine - Dey run to God wid lips

H. E. Krehbiel and others have explored the ranges of several spirituals. In some respects, certain of the spirituals were instrumental in character, departing from diatonicism and other vocal idioms in general. Some of the greatest intervalic leaps were found in *I Just Been to the Fountain, No Man Can Hinder Me* and *O'er the Crossing* (Ex. 11). The slaves were naturally influenced by remnants of the practices of their own ancestors, some of whose songs contained melodic ranges at least as wide as octaves. Coupled with the highly ornamental performance of an African heritage, these collections indicated a history of great talent.

Texture

Original spirituals were not created in the same manner as the tonal concert arrangements so familiar today, complete with brilliant piano accompaniments. The oldest of spirituals were often vocal, with or without instrumental accompaniment, depending upon the occasion. They were either melodic compositions performed by a single soloist, or were harmonies composed at random with a melody begun by a leader. Harmony was improvised by singers at hand, and consisted of an amalgamation of African and European sounds. Undoubtedly, this resulted in both homophonic and polyphonic compositions. The homophonic types were similar in style to hymns, having two to four parts. This style contained a leader whose main melody was supported by two and/or four-part harmony.

Afro-American compositions were also quasi-pholyphonic or imitative in style. Performances of such pieces were the results of antiphonal or "call and response" singing between solo and chorus or between ensemble and ensemble. The same themes or different melodies altogether were sung by the choruses, and alternations of the phrases sometimes overlapped. This polyphony was close to "canons" or other small pieces of the early Baroque, but were not as imitative or intricate as those of the later Baroque period.

Not only was polyphony realized by vocal timbres, but accompanying instruments added to this complexity of overlapping sounds. With their many varieties of rhythms in contrapuntal style, they developed a definitive position of African polyphony. Example 13a shows an African example in contrast to an example of Afro-American music.

Ex. 13a. African and American polyphony. *Osenyee bobuo ee* (Condolences), No. 28, *Folk Songs* by J. K. Nketia. Used by Permission of African Institute, University of Ghana at Legon.

Ex. 13b. *Sittin' Down Beside O' The Lamb*, taken from *American Negro Songs and Spirituals*, edited by John W. Work. © 1940 by John W. Work. Used by permission of Crown Publishers, Inc.

Ornamentation in Spirituals

The body of spirituals contained a wide variety of ornaments derived from African vocal music. Just as Africans had decorated their bodies for dance and their instruments for effects, so had they maintained a continuous tradition of vocal decoration. Early explorers wrote of this fascinating

32

aspect of African music before American colonialism, and the practice did not end with the arrival of Africans in America. Aside from rhythmic influence, improvised inflections of African origin have influenced American music more than any other element.

Although some transcriptions did not reflect ornaments (such as the *Slave Songs* by Ware, etc.) Harold Courlander gave clearer insight into the traditional manner of performance. Since Blacks have seemingly always had a tradition of improvising an innocent melody, the Courlander collection, *Negro Songs from Alabama* showed how vocal approximations must have been sung. E. A. McIlhenny, who claimed to have copied his harmonies as Blacks sang them, gave his information about ornamentation in his collection of *Befo' de War Spirituals*. Reared in America and having observed the singing of slaves as a child, McIlhenny frequently sat in church where the songs were performed. He wrote:

> It is almost impossible to get exact wording of spirituals for even the same singer never sings one twice exactly the same. The singer will vary the words, lines and melody every time . . . . Stanzas never occur twice in the same order, but are sung as they come to the mind of the singer, and as the singer will improvise . . . the number of stanzas . . . is unlimited . . . . There is also great variation . . . begins with a simple sweet melody, but as the singer becomes more . . . uplifted and enthused by oft repeated lines, all sorts of quavering notes and melodious expression will be improvised.

One characteristic style governed by an emotional state, boasted the art of "hitting" a note from each side by sliding into and away from it, thereby not exacting a given pitch. A difficult technique within itself, this manner of singing resembled a wavering or trill-like technique, and in other situations, a slide or approximation at best. Some have recorded the same techniques in examples of African music, thus providing examples of African ornamentation.

Rhythmic groups such as triplets, dotted figures and sixteenth notes also served to ornament the vocal line. Turns (e.g. notes sung above and below the main notes, but not necessarily changing tones as in western music), auxiliary tones and other additions were sung using these rhythmic groups. *Job, Job,* and *Preach My Gospel,* of the Harold Courlander collection, *Poor Mourner's Got a Home at Last* and *This Is a Sin-Tryin' World* of the John W. Work collection and various African counterparts from the Nketia and Jones' collections demonstrate the traditions of added notes and vocal inflections. One of these, *Preach My Gospel,* strongly resembles the highly melismatic style of certain ancient western Gregorian chants in that the vocal line is so ornamented that a great distortion of the words results in the extension of syllables. Some of the rhythmic ornaments are seen in Example 14, but as in the case of other musical elements, should be considered as approximate.

Ex. 14.   Ornaments in spirituals.

a.   b.   c.   d.   e. Michael row de boat ashore...

Due to oral tradition which allowed differences in numerous versions of the same song, the use of ornaments and improvisation resulted in still other versions. The familiar *Nobody Knows, Were You There?* and *Go Down Moses* were but three songs which could be heard as follows:

Ex. 15. Variations in spirituals.

a. Versions I: *Nobody Knows; Go Down, Moses; Were You There?*
b. Versions II: Alternates of same compositions.

Rhythm

One of the most direct influences of Africa was found in the diverse and difficult rhythms of spirituals. Based upon the rhythms of drum and dance as well as emotional spontaneity, they spun into movements which encouraged foot reactions similar to the contagion of jazz as well as vocal communion among the slave population. Inherent within the spirituals were such dance rhythms as the shout, the bamboula and both religious and secular influences. Depending upon the spirits of the people, these rhythms were either heavy and somber, or gay and carefree. Although a few of the meters were transcribed into triple rhythm, the majority of the spirituals were performed in the duple meter of the shout. The rhythm of a spiritual as shown in Example 16 incorporates both the movement of the shout and of the glorious spirit within the song.

Ex. 16. *Shout on Chil'en* from *Slave Songs* by Allen, Garrison & Ware.

Shout on, chil'en, you never die; Glory hallelu!
You in de Lord, an' de Lord in you; Glory hallelu!

Although simple, regular meters did exist in the collections mentioned, the bulk were irregular or uncommon combinations of six and two together, or of three and two. Most of the meters in duple time did not affect syncopations, short and long phrases of rhythmic sequences, or alternations from six to three, etc.

Unlike the African examples of rhythm which were governed by the text and generally changed when words differed, American songs were more repetitive in their renditions. Many American versions were repetitive for two reasons: First, many songs were created on the spot without much time for serious or formal alterations; second, there was the problem of a limited vocabulary in a foreign tongue. Yet the popularity of some songs had to depend partly on simplicity and their ability to be learned quickly. On the other hand, some of the more sophisticated, refreshing examples of story-telling spirituals were more verbose, indicating that many had been composed during leisure hours or over long periods of time. Such examples could also suggest a talented, educated leader or trained musician.

As in African music, the text was the significant element in the effect of Afro-American music. Yet the newer texts created some problems of juxtaposition with the music and therefore the text eventually lost the original fluidity and natural beauty of the African languages. The harder sounds of emerging dialects of European languages replaced the soft, fluid and musical quality inherent in the African languages. Consequently, inflections of new words in the melodic line were lost due to rhythmic awkwardness.

Tempos were fast, moderate and slow, depending on the emotions emitted by the text. However, one tempo was not necessarily "reserved" for a religious piece as opposed to one for a secular text. Depending upon the function and the mood of both the group and the situation at hand, tempos would change to meet the event. In such cases, tempos were as relative or as obscure as an "allegro" or an "adagio" of western examples. They were learned and performed according to the whims of the leader, and varied from performance to performance.

Rhythmic cadences ended either on long or short notes suggested by the mood and character of the pieces. *God Got Plenty of Room, Rock O' Jubilee, Tell My Jesus Mornin', No Man Can Hinder Me* and others represented in the *Slave Songs* by Ware, Garrison and Allen, indicate short endings. The majority of spirituals, however, used the traditional endings of western music. The following spirituals reveal African-American rhythms and when compared with the chart of African rhythms found in Chapter II, encompass many of the characteristics seen in the preceding discussion.

Ex. 17. Rhythm in spirituals.

I Got a home up in-a that Kingdom, (Ain't-a That Good News!)

(I Got Shoes;) You got shoes; All-a God's Chil'en got shoes!
When I get to Heaven, gonna put on m'shoes an' gonna shout
all over God's Heaven!

Fier, my Saviour, fier; Satan's Camp A-fire;
Fier, believer, fier, (Satan's Camp A-fire).

Form

The most common poetry was shaped into four lines with a refrain. Four to six lines or more were also seen. There was the ballad form, variation form, binary form (as seen in *Lonesome Valley* and *Praise Member*), ternary form, strophic and other patterns of altered forms. There were also pieces which appeared to be through-composed.

Spirituals sometimes resembled blues or ballads and could be distinguished by the text and manner of spirit. For example, some blues contained from three to six or more lines of poetry while the spirituals customarily contained four lines. Some similarities in poetic construction were seen in *I Wish to God, Steady, Jesus Listenin'* and the others compared below:

I.   Four lines (Blues)   (Spiritual)

I wish to God that train would come,	Steady, Jesus listenin',
I wish to God that train would come,	Steady, Jesus listenin',
I wish to God that train would come,	Steady, Jesus listenin',
To take me back where I come from.	You must be born again.

II.   Three lines (Blues)   (Spiritual)

I rushed down there, but a little too late,	Dere's no rain to wet you,
I rushed down there, but a little too late,	Oh yes, I want to go home.
Thief had got my chickens and made it for the gate.	Want to go home.

In particular, the call and response technique of the leader and chorus influenced almost all of the spirituals. Few were composed, according to available sources, without leaders. The chorus responded in repetitious phrases, leaving a soloist free to compose words as the song progressed. As a definite feature of African formations, one or two singers could lead the chorus into any of the following alternatives:

I.   Call and Response Techniques

Verse:	Solo	First Line	or:	Solo I
	Chorus	Second Line		Solo II
	Solo	Third Line		Solo I
	Chorus	Fourth Line		Solo II
Refrain:		Tutti		Tutti

II.   Call and Response Techniques

Verse:	Chorus	First Line	or:	Tutti
	Solo	Second Line		Solo
	Chorus	Third Line		Chorus
	Solo	Fourth Line		Chorus
Refrain:	Tutti			Solo

36

Example 18 gives both African and Afro-American techniques which further point to the frequency of the call and response:

Ex. 18. Call and response in Africa and America.
Ayirem obi barima, No. 4, from *Folk Songs of Ghana* by J. K. Nketia. Used by permission of the composer.

Oh Mary, O Martha, Traditional.

Timbre

Since tradition consisted of vocal and instrumental ensembles along with dancing, there is reason to believe that many varieties of instrumental timbres existed, even if not as frequently practiced as in African concepts. Unquestionably, spirituals mainly represented a vocal style of great emotion.

A rarity in print is an instrumental version of a song entitled *Prayer,* which follows in the style of vocal spirituals. This clever example was found in Alabama and reveals a genuine spirit of a by-gone era.

Ex. 19. *Prayer*, No. 8, from *Negro Songs from Alabama* by Harold Courlander, author and collector; transcribed by John Benson Brooks. Used by permission.

Originality of Spirituals

The originality of spirituals by Blacks has been the subject of much scrutiny and criticism as well as commendation. In 1863, Frederick Ritter stated the "merit" of the songs. Still others felt that they consisted of too much borrowing and were therefore not original at all. Dr. Richard Wallenschek, in *An Inquiry into the Origin and Development of Music, Songs, Instruments, Dances and Pantomimes of Savage Races,* voiced the opinion that "Negro songs were very much overrated" and that they were "mere imitations of European compositions which the Negroes had picked up and served up again with only slight variation".

A statement so misleading as both the title and the thought should not go unchallenged, for any composer has always deserved the right to use elements which he has heard. The art of musical composition has frequently consisted of borrowing from generations long ago to the era of television commercials today. The practice of using another composer's material for thematic inspiration and improvisation has been noted throughout the history of both classical and popular music. Popular melodies once served as "cantus firmi", or principal melodies around which other parts were woven to create religious works. Other examples have occurred in the theme and variations form from Handel to Brahms and imitative pieces of Bach. The borrowed melody was often altered or so changed or interwoven until detection was almost impossible. These classical ideas and their use and variation were the tools of the master artist.

While it was true that some elements of White songs of America influenced early Black composers, it was equally true that African-Americans borrowed from their own native land to provide themselves with materials. It was also a fact that in their process of alteration there resulted a complete change in the music, as discussed above, and such improvisation rendered the songs quite unique. This was particularly true in cases where African texts were translated into English or French, or where examples were altered by additions or rhythmic excitements. The late John Work III, a noted teacher-composer, staunchly defended this right to provide, produce and reproduce. He also proved how much the final result differed from the originals.

As it was noticed that American slaves were great imitators of the music about them, so did Ware, Allen and Garrison, in the preface of their *Slave Songs,* notice that a few of the slave songs recorded in their book became established favorites among Whites as well. They noted that hardly a Sunday passed at the church on St. Helena without the use of *Gabriel's Trumpet, I Heard from Heaven Today* or *Jehovah Hallejah.* However, the songs undoubtedly took on a contrary meaning to Whites and were not the same as when sung by Blacks. For it was a fact that the burdens, hardships and inconveniences reflected in many of the songs could not possibly have been realized to their fullest extent by those who had not suffered the same injustices.

History has also shown that White composers have borrowed Black materials from African concepts of performance and construction from minstrelsy to jazz and from tin pan alley to popular. Stephen Foster, Dan Emmett, Thomas Rice, George Gershwin and a host of others used materials lifted directly from the ballads and life patterns of Blacks for use in their own compositions. Part III will discuss other kindred materials during the contemporary era, consisting of composers such as Aaron Copland, Igor Stravinsky and Darius Milhaud. Those who once criticized Blacks so harshly of borrowing melodies hardly ever wrote of this reverse fact, and books since that time which failed to reflect the history of Black contributions to American and other music have committed a "sin of omission" by unwittingly omitting facts as to the roots of some American music.

In addition to the above anonymous "composers" of untrained skills, it must be realized that there were a few exceptions of Blacks who were capable of composing thoughtful works of art. Some Black concert artists performed music of all kinds at an early time and were capable of reading music. They traveled in America and in Europe, along with those in America who were either free men or slave plantation performers. At a later time, those Blacks located around larger cities as New Orleans were better able to read and write music at an earlier age than were the most unsophisticated field hands. There were doubtless several of these who were musicians as talented as the Black Euro-African violinist and composer, George Bridgetower, whose concert associations with Ludwig Beethoven were favorable and real.

Influence of the Spirituals

Spirituals became artistic forms during the era of Reconstruction and were made famous by the pioneer performances of the Fisk Jubilee Singers. Unable to appreciate the worth of the songs, they were at first reluctant to promote the excellence of compositional techniques with emotion. Could the Afro-Americans have been ashamed to sing songs to the God of their oppressors? Or had they not been freed by the same God? Was this an intellectual rebuff against the hateful conditions of slave art, or disgust for the circumstances? And finally, why could these songs serve Blacks in slavery but not at the time of their release?

Art had always been practical for the African, and it was partly so for the Afro-American. It was not something separate and opposite from life, an object away from his being as afforded only by the elite, erudite and rich. His idea of the functioning art was perhaps responsible for the fact that certain of his songs were buried and forgotten after Emancipation, having outgrown their purpose. He no longer felt the need for *Steal Away* in quite the same way as had Nat Turner, the minister-insurrectionist, and perhaps the composer of the song. Now the Afro-American wished to retain only that which was free — free of anything peculiar to the illusions and institutions of slavery.

Fortunately, the Fisk Singers were finally persuaded to sing the spirituals in order to raise funds for the school, not then a university. The sincere desire for the continuation of their education inspired them to abandon former prejudices against the spirituals and to promote the depths of emotions found within these long rejected compositions. Since then, spirituals enlightened the world to their messages and emotions, becoming the penetrating force in both popular and classical music of the modern period.

One of the more popular spirituals, *No More Auction Block For Me* (*Many Thousand Gone*) was paraphrased in the song *We Shall Overcome,* a protest form of the 1960's. Arrangements and adaptations of spirituals have also been recorded in abundance for concert solo and choral ensembles, having been promoted since the era of the Jubilee Singers by com-

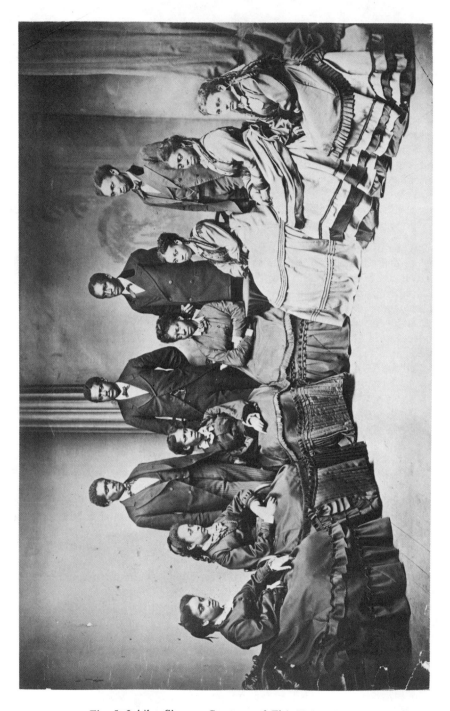

Fig. 5. Jubilee Singers. Courtesy of Fisk University.

posers Nathaniel Dett, John W. Work III, Eva Jessye, Margaret Bond, William Dawson, Undine Moore, the Johnsons, H. T. Burleigh and many others. Symphonies and other compositions have been written utilizing the characteristics of these songs. It was Burleigh's singing of spirituals, for instance, that gave way to the inspirations for the Czech composer, Anton Dvorak, to complete his *New World Symphony*. Other composers such as William Grant Still and William Dawson have composed music based on spirituals.

In turn, Whites in America have also studied and used elements of spirituals in search of Americanism. Inspired by Dvorak's *Symphony,* they pursued indigenous music of the American Indian and the Black American in hopes of capturing the spirit of American nationalism in music, popular during the late nineteenth century. Indeed, the wealth of melodic intricacies and rhythmic motives fascinated most American composers at one time or another. The influence of spirituals is found in the following compositions which represent but a sample of their power, a fundamental basis for many styles to come:

Afro-American Suite, Undine Moore, for flute, cello, piano
Afro-American Symphony, William Grant Still, for orchestra
Negro Folk Symphony, William Dawson, for orchestra
25 Negro Spirituals, Samuel Coleridge-Taylor, for piano

PART TWO

THE AWAKENING (1870's-1950's)

V
MODERN PERIOD:
EMERGENCE OF BLACK PROFESSIONALS

African-Americans emerged in the late 1800's as professionals in many areas from scientific research to artistic achievements. Although greatly experimental, strides were nevertheless made in publishing and performance, academic and business ventures and in status changes. Having gained momentum from the days of Nat Turner, this era boasted some brilliant leaders whose philosophies and general contributions helped shape the music and the lives of Black people for successive generations. Of considerable influence were the philosopher-educators W. E. B. DuBois, Frederick Douglas, Marcus Garvey and Booker T. Washington. Their collective theories showed the Black position as it existed then and denoted needs and goals to be met.

By 1900, America produced many scholars in philosophy, poetry, science, art and music. Some of the most illuminating of Black poets were found in Harlem, New York — Langston Hughes, James Weldon Johnson and Countee Cullen. Countless musicians such as Louis Armstrong and Duke Ellington also contributed to the era. Their accomplishments were referred to as the "Black Renaissance" and were designed to point out, defend and promote the talents and worth of the Black man and his culture.

Erupting out of the violent slave era, this second stage of Black development was formed against the transition from the European Romantic period, American Reconstruction and Africanism to the dilemmas of the World War, Modernism and Black assimilation. Affected by the psychological, physical and social elements of the society which prevailed in a segregated society, these Americans were little better off in "knowing their place" of race and class status than they were previously. This colored the conditions within which the music was composed, and confused natural growth of emotional reactions. Thus all did not run smoothly for these recently freed slaves regardless of this professionalism.

If Leroi Jones' *Blues People* felt that the earliest part of Black American history reflected a shout and an expression of the blues, so did these more modern problems of economics, social errors, poverty and power struggles also sustain the "blue" ingredients of life. Perhaps the requirements of urban living over rural life, or the almost complete relocation of the New Orleans musicians contributed to the everpresent complexities of an overcrowded profession. Eventually, countless musicians moved into

45

the larger cities from many localities. They were either able to "sell their wares" more readily, or were not able to sell them at all.

The blues followed Blacks into urban environments as faithfully and persistently as spirituals followed slaves to the plantation. Nowhere was there a hiding place. The great congregations of people who had moved from the south lured by northern opportunities in technology as well as in the arts, were frequently the last to be hired and the first to be fired. Jobs were hard to find, and hard to keep, and the social plights were equally unjust. Consequently, many had to work under the precarious conditions of the speakeasy, and at the whims of racketeers. In addition, jobs were not fairly distributed among Blacks and Whites, thus eliminating or limiting the rapid growth of Black professionalism in the arts.

Some blues related the sadness found in the treatment and conditions of Blacks. *I'm Tired of Bein' Jim Crowed, Cloudy in the West* and other blues which depicted poverty, depression and despair were found in abundance, and stressed the downhearted facts of life from "I spent my last nickel in a subway train . ." to "I gave up my room, could not pay the rent; went down to the Welfare and didn't get a cent".

No matter that they did not find the economic security which they so desperately needed, the majority of Black professionals ultimately profited by remaining in an urban setting. Many found fame in publishing and recording, radio appearances, night clubs and concert halls. Musicians also found limited but supportive aid from the Works Progress Administration (WPA), a federal organization established during the depression which helped supply jobs for many urban citizens.

Not only were American cities advantageous to the musician, but concepts and studies abroad in such cities as Paris were possible. These deeper commitments to the music produced a better prepared individual who grew to achieve popular notoriety in swing, bebop and other jazz styles as well as that of the classical arts.

The history of Black professionalism in America rested heavily upon the musical experiences which Blacks had inherited and practiced for innumerable decades. According to Robert Stevenson, their African ancestors had perfected the art of music in their societies as early as the seventh century, and had traveled to share their findings with nearby Asian and European countries. In America, Blacks had also performed as slaves and free men dating back to the 1700's and possibly before. However, there had been little or no gain economically, as many slaves had been hired out by the lure of mere trinkets for themselves while their "masters" received the money. Paid Blacks were few indeed. This new era in the history of Black professionalism therefore marked the time when more significant numbers of Blacks generally outlined their own careers and participated in commercial undertakings for the benefit of their own fame and fortune.

VI
BLACK MINSTRELS

The history of Black minstrels began in Africa and descended into Afro-American lifestyles of early colonial times. Many of the characteristics observed in early Black minstrelsy were similar to those from Europe, while others were quite different. In the *Harvard Dictionary of Music,* Apel defined minstrels as "professional musicians of the Middle Ages, especially those who were employed in a feudal household" and "of show business activities and the music thereof." These European-based minstrels, called minnesingers, troubadours, trouveres or jongleurs, performed as jugglers, acrobats, poetic debaters, tricksters and musicians.

Particularly since the publishing of Frank Snowden's book, *Blacks in Antiquity,* we now know that some of those minstrels who performed in ancient Europe were Africans. In fact, the idea of such minstrels was also found in Africa long before the Middle Ages and decidedly long before our American roots were established. A report of West African minstrels, called "griots" by D. T. Niane, showed similarities to those in Europe. Found in *Sundiata, An Epic of Old Mali,* it outlined duties of the traveling griots whose oral tradition ranged from preserving and verbalizing historical records, recalling lineages and engaging in the counseling of kings to playing magical tricks and musical instruments.

Blacks served as traveling minstrels in America before 1800. Particularly after Reconstruction, Black minstrels participated in shows which traveled from city to city in search of money and fame. Alternating their acts with songs, dances, jokes, dialogues and clowning, they differed from earlier jesters in that the painted face represented that of the Black American. Unlike the clown who mixed his colors to depict emotions of comic gaity and distortion, and unlike the African who used his colors to similate colors with human emotions (white, for example, denoted joy) this use of the charcoal color was not for similar ceremonies.

Colored faces eventually became a compulsory rule for the American minstrel shows. An obnoxious practice begun by Whites and subsequently demanded by audiences of both races, many Blacks were forced to continue it for the sake of popularity. This cyclic force of the White man painting his face to resemble a despised Black was therefore copied by the Black man himself, an irony of comedy personified.

Judging a blackface as a performer in imitation of a Black man was ludicrous in itself. Taking another view, it was excruciatingly painful and

47

humiliating to enjoy a living while enduring that predicament. However, even if Blacks felt themselves "traitors" in bowing to unkind demands, who could blame them for a sense of economic justice in the quest for an honest living? And who could blame them for claiming a share of a fame so readily available?

Music, on the other hand, was an artistic expression which was not always looked upon as something as evil as the society in which it grew. For one thing, Black minstrels proved to be as talented, skillful and enjoyable as their competitors, and secondly, their shows were hilariously comical. Because comedy and talent were in command of the audiences, Black minstrels soon learned to subdue the uncomfortable realities and to smile through the medium of song. Consequently, music eventually overcame the demeaning sneers and coerced the performers to laugh with the audience.

Origins of American Minstrelsy

Because American minstrelsy was a type of staged production which flourished from early 1800 to early 1900, it was one of the oldest settings for Black professionals. Its commercial authority embraced the life of Stephen Foster (1826-1864) and terminated near the death of a famous Black counterpart, James Bland (1854-1911). Even though the late Alain Locke, philosopher and writer, divided minstrelsy into two parts (1850-1875 and 1875-1895), it is obvious that the fact functioned well outside these dates, having begun with early colonial life and eventually directed toward vaudeville, burlesque, extravaganza, or the "tin pan" varieties of modern music.

Legend and fact showed that Blacks were responsible for the embryonic stages of American minstrelsy, and that many were involved in musical contributions as to form, style, instrumentation and performance practices. Ever since Blacks were commanded to "make a noise" in the field or were invited to perform at plantation revelries, their skills have inspired subjects and patterns for secondhand presentations among Whites. Blacks, however, could not claim the credit for American commercialism of the art, since exploitation of their ideas first benefited others.

Although the origins of American minstrelsy were not generally recorded as having been contributed by Blacks, the popular story about Thomas Rice (1808-1860) did confirm that he had imitated on stage a song and dance routine which he had copied from a deformed Black. Also printed in Christy's *Minstrel Songster,* it stated in part:

Come listen all you gals and boys,
I'se just from Tacky Hoe,
I'm goin' to sing a little song;
My name's Jim Crow! (*Several verses*)

Chorus
Wheel about an' turn about an' do jus' so;
Ebry time I wheel about I jump Jim Crow!

48

Little did that Black man know that he would jump Jim Crow for so long thereafter, for not only was this JC routine carried out on stage but offstage as well. "Jim Crowism" became a sensational act to be repeated time and time again, with thunderous applause from a separated society. And little did America know that the Black man's deformity would shape the disfigurement of the Nation for so long a time. It was significant that "Jim Crow" was later used to describe segregation in all of its manifestations. Thus, minstrels also implied segregation, in spite of the joy of its musical worth.

Media and Minstrel Participants

Much as in opera, instruments were used for introductions, interludes, postludes and accompaniment. The familiar solos, duets and choruses joined with the banjo, piano, guitar, gongs, tambourines, and other percussions and winds. Later, the band instrumentation was developed into small ragtime ensembles.

Near 1800, a poster of the era listed the following instruments required: tuba, banjo, violin, clappers, bass and viola. No doubt, there was not a set instrumentation, as performances were accorded by both taste and available instruments. The same poster read:

Needed:

1. musician to double band and orchestra; bass drummer who reads; trombone, baritone, all must double.
2. wanted: bass singer for quartette, doubling comedy, etc., strong cornet player . . .
3. one strong colored cornet player . . . salary must be low (!)

Minstrel participants depended upon the instruments to support their actions from beginning to end. These participants ranged from the announcer or interlocutor who was frequently interrupted with spasmodic chords from the band, to the end men or blackface comedians. The stump speakers, Tambo and Mr. Bones, were also an expected part of the show since they alternately fed each other ridiculous, and sometimes ribald, jokes along with the "brer rabbit" type stories. Other characters were arranged as soloists, choruses and other small ensembles with dances assembled on stage.

Form

The overall form of the show resembled an operetta in that its main elements of dance, spoken dialogue and song were similarly written. While the operetta was most related to the opera because of its quality of music drama, the minstrel show was not necessarily a story, but rather a series of events arranged into scenes and acts. It was a variety show whose unsophisticated presentations covered the activities of the south, with particular emphasis upon southern Blacks. One example of a show was seen in *Dusky Clouds* by Nahaves and Lippmann, whose program of events was:

1. Overture (instrumental)
2. Opening chorus
3. Song (solo with chorus)
4. *Carry Me Back to Old Virginny* (dance music by J. Bland)
5. Song (male quartet)
6. Song (waltz, ballad)
7. Song (company)
8. Scarf dance (specialty)
9. Song (solo with chorus)
10. Finale (company)

Some forms within the shows included European dances such as the waltz. There were also early Afro-American routines such as the cakewalk, an elaborate strutting effect; the shuffle, the buck and wing, the clog, the jig, the pigeon wing and others. Later, there were tap dances, rags, camel walk, turkey trots, grizzly bear and the lame duck, which became popular even in vaudeville shows. Still others represented in song forms were the airs, ballads, blues and hybrid forms, the most important of which are discussed in the following sections.

Ballads, Blues and Hybrids

Two of the most popular song forms of Black minstrelsy were the ballad and the blues. The ballad, a romantic or sentimental song, told a story or expressed an emotion in short, simple stanzas, and was quite similar to the earlier European poetry depicting romance and exciting adventures. The blues reflected despair and sadness, but really contained commentaries of several moods from depression and self-pity to love and cynicism. Generally a style of either verse with refrain, or verse without refrain, it could also contain humorous words similar to those of some ballads. Both types used an ABAB structure with choral refrains ABAC and ABAB repeated, and they occurred with verses and refrains reversed. Many varieties existed as simple airs, or even as "da capo". Some ballads were also AABB with refrain or in ABA form. Both forms were tonal structures, in keeping with nineteenth century practices.

The ballad spoke of the same subjects as the blues — love, places, people and things. Its words, however, were generally happier in content, outlook and presentation, and contained close styles with the European songs. Not always sophisticated, ballads were apt to use euphemism in their expressions, were more verbose and frequently through-composed. On the other hand, blues were more often concerned with the raw and real bluntness of life, and would state messages with unsophisticated earthiness. The blues form was generally repetitious in its texts, even though the shape and structure were not always of the classic twelve-bar type. A similarity of ideas is seen in the comparison of the ballad and blues tests below, as well as a difference in word formations:

50

Ballad:
Carry me back to ole Virginny.
There's where the cotton and
   'tatoes grow . . .
There's where this ole darkey's
   heart am long'd to go.

Blues:
I've got those Vicksburg blues
   and I'm singin' it everywhere I please.
Now, the reason I'm singin' it
   is to give my poor heart
   some ease.

Some ballad texts not necessarily composed for the minstrel shows were nevertheless influential. Some were of the mixed blues-ballad types, or hybrids. Others were free varieties such as catchy ditties of the street or playground. One such example was *Hard to Be a Nigger*:

Naught fer naught, figger fer figger,
Figger fer de white man, Naught fer de nigger!

Another example was *Short'nin Bread*:

Two little niggers lyin' in bed,
One of 'em sick an' de odder mos' dead.
Call fer de doctor an' de doctor said,
Feed dem darkies on short'nin' bread.

While ballads resembled blues, some of the words also were related to spirituals and other songs. One verse used in the shows came from *When de Good Lord Sets You Free,* whose likeness was akin to *Shortnin' Bread*:

Big Black nigger, lyin' on de log,
Finger on de trigger, eye on de hog.
Gun say bump! Hog say bip!
Nigger jumped on him with all his grip.

The chorus of the same song was less secular in its text, and reflected the religious elements so typical in the songs of Black folks: "Oh mourner, you shall be free . . ."

Hybrid ballads were further influenced by the spirituals. The following song shows religious and secular texts in *Cornfield Medley*:

Well I heard a mighty rumblin' an' I didn't know from where,
From way down yonder in the cornfiel'.
T'was only brother Gabriel just a-combin' out his hair
From way down yonder in the cornfiel'.

51

Chorus:
Tra la la la la la la *(repeat)*
Oh sinners, it won't be long,

Solo:
Till you hear brother Gabriel go up in the cloud and say . . .

Chorus:
Peter, go ring dem bells *(repeat)*
I heard from heav'n to hail, hail, hail, Jerusalem, hail!
Maha, ha, Hail, Jerusalem, Hail . . . . etc.

In addition to resembling one of the songs listed in *Callender's Original Minstrel Songsters,* the above also had representations from the spiritual, *Dere's a Meetin' Here Tonight.*

Early Composer-performers

Composers of minstrelsy were most often performers. Therefore, the history of performance involved the art of composition, whether or not it was transcribed. Frequently, the oral tradition was used to preserve Black compositions because neither Blacks nor Whites could notate the music exactly. Consequently, many bards went unrecorded in history, since few manuscripts carried the name of the Black composer. One such musically inclined person sought to correct this injustice by partially identifying himself:

Ef anybody ax you who writ dis song,
Tell 'im 'twuz a dark-skinned nigger
Wid a pair o' blue duckins on,
A-lookin' for a home,
Jes a-lookin' for a home.

Many tunes actually composed by Blacks were written down by Whites. The work of Thomas Ricc was one example. Other Whites who served as 'keepers of records' were Stephen Foster, whose *Ring, Ring de Banjo, Old Black Joe* and *My Kentucky Home* were inspired by Black subjects. *Ethiopian Walk-Around* by Dan Emmett, was later adopted by Confederate Whites as their *Dixie.*

Perhaps the first noteworthy Black writer of popular ballads was Samuel Lucas (1848-1916). His *Grandfather's Clock Is Too Tall for the Shelf* (which has also been attributed to H. C. Work), and his *Carve Dat Possum* were favorites among the people. Along with Billy Kersands and James Bland, he was considered among the greatest of "comedian-writers." At that time, composers, comedians, dancers etc. were expected to double in their performances; thus earning that title. Most, however, did not necessarily carry the title of composer or singer during early minstrelsy, since the word "minstrel" was inseparable from the various other duties of composer-performer.

Many composers of minstrelsy were represented in early jazz in some reports, e.g., A. J. R. Connor, composer of *My Cherished Hope, My Fondest Dreams, American Polka Quadrilles, New York Polka Waltz* and others; Gussie Davis, composer of *In the Baggage Coach Ahead, Do the Old Folks Miss Me, My Creole Sue, Down in Poverty Row, The Fatal Wedding, The Light House by the Sea, When Nelly Was Raking the Hay, Wait 'Til the Tide Comes In, The Cabin on the Mississippi Shore;* Nathan Bivens, composer of *It Makes no Dif'rence What You Do, Get the Money;* Will Accooe, composer of *'Cause I'se in Society Now, A Trip to Coon Town;* and George Milburn, composer of *Listen to the Mocking Bird.* As in the case of the latter composer, many Blacks sold their rights to the songs which they composed, thus contributing to the difficulty in tracing their origins.

THOMAS (BLIND TOM) BETHUNE (1849-1908)

Thomas Bethune, composer-pianist, was born a slave near Columbus, Georgia. One of the most colorful of the early writers, he was a child prodigy variously described as "a genius with unerring memory" or an eccentric. He has also been described as an "oddity" or an "idiotic" person perhaps mainly because of his daily physical exercises which must have resembled Yoga, and because of the self-punishment inflicted upon his eyes in an attempt to gain his eyesight — a practice which sometimes resulted in the success of capturing glimpses of obscured images and light. No one can ridicule, however, the documented writings which speak of his largely self-taught ability and inspiration to excel on a near-miracle level of achievement.

A widely acclaimed concert pianist, he was early tested by professional musicians and discovered to be a most brilliant musician with perfect pitch who could duplicate perfectly on the piano any music which was played for him. His owner exhibited his talents in concerts throughout the United States, Africa and Europe, where his performances included nearly 5,000 catalogued pieces from Chopin and Beethoven to his own original works. The Moorland Room at Howard University houses written attestations to these facts of his "profound sensationalism" and the Azalia Hackley Room at Detroit supports these facts through various newspapers and exhibitions of his published works.

Of a tonal style which reflected the theoretical practices of the nineteenth century and salon-type descriptions of the natural resources around him, his compositions included *Rainstorm, The Battle of Manassas* and others.

JAMES BLAND (1854-1911)

One of the most famous, talented, entertaining and exciting of the early Black composer-performers was James Bland. Born in Flushing, New York, Bland spent much of his life in Philadelphia and Washington, attending Washington public schools. According to his biographer, John Daly, he enrolled at Howard University for a short time, studied theory

53

Fig. 6. James Bland. Courtesy of Virginia State Library.

with a Professor White and later abandoned his education in order to join with the Haverly Colored Minstrels who were performing in Baltimore. A newspaper article found in the Azalia Hackley Collection Room in Detroit's Public Library, however, stated that Bland graduated from Howard. He then left America for Europe where he became quite famous and lived well above his means. Squandering his money and neglecting his health led to his decline. By the time he returned to America, he was forgotten and was not offered adequate work to maintain his expenses.

According to John Daly, Bland was credited with making the "Bland Banjo," a five-stringed instrument thought to be a combination of African derivation plus the violin fingerboard. However, Bland was not the originator of the banjo, according to John Tasker Howard. He credited its creation to another Black, Joel Walker Sweeney (1813-1860) who, in imitation of the gourd banjo used by the slaves, stretched some skin across a cheesebox and placed five strings on it. Howard pointed out that many believed this to be a myth. However, it was a fact that the history of the African "gonje" (a gourd with strings) and the harp or any of the stringed instruments common to Africa testified to the credibility of this matter. In

54

fact, to make such an instrument would not have been difficult for the slaves. Bland was nevertheless significant in making improvements upon the original banjo, no matter who created it.

Like Stephen Foster, his white counterpart, Bland wrote over 700 songs, many of which were not recorded and were consequently lost, stolen, or sold. As was the case in art music, both publishers and composers of the day were dishonest, careless and impractical in the matter of copyrights, and were generally unprofessional. Also like Foster, Bland was born into a well-to-do family, whose father was the first Black to hold the position of Examiner in the United States Patent Office. Both Foster and Bland were said by Daly to have led wild and reckless lives, and both were nearly fifty when they died. Neither was a good business man, and each allowed his money to slip away.

Among the most famous of the songs which Bland wrote were *Carry Me Back to Ole Virginny,* adopted by the State of Virginia in 1940 as the State Song, and *Oh Dem Golden Slippers,* both themes of which are shown below. It is also significant that *Carry Me Back to Ole Virginny* is found in the old *Christy Minstrel Songster* as a song composed by another Black, Charles White. However, it is seemingly similar in title only.

Ex. 20. *Carry Me Back to Ole Virginny* and *Oh Dem Golden Slippers.* Permission granted by Theodore Presser Company.

1. Car-ry me back to old Vir-gin-ny, There's where the cot ton and the corn and 'ta-toes grow,

1. Oh my gold-en slip-pers am laid a-way, Kas' I don't 'spect to wear 'em till my wed-din' day,

His other pieces were various types of ballads, musicals and airs. His writing was similar to that of Foster, especially as to the subject of texts, the general emotional styles and his use of basic chord structures. Sometimes through-composed pieces, they were mostly strophic form, having verses with choral refrains, or vice versa. In part, his list of compositions included: *Close Dem Windows, Hand Me Down My Walking Stick, Listen to the Silver Trumpet, Dancing on De Kitchen Floor, Oh, Lucinda, The Homestead, Father's Growing Old, Missouri Hound Dog, Hot Time in Our Town, In the Evening by the Moonlight, Pretty Little Caroline Rose, De Golden Wedding, You could have Been True, Gabriel's Band, The Old Fashion-Cottage, The Farmer's Daughter, Christmas Dinner, You Gotta Stop Kicking My Hound Around, Dandy Black Brigade, There's a Long, Long, Trail, Heaven Is My Harbor, In the Morning by the Bright Light, Listen to the Silver Trumpets, Keep Dem Golden Gates Wide Open* and a musical, *Sporting Girl.*

Later Composers

Black composers of the 1900's made more sophisticated effects, drawing from the experiences of the rag and other existing varieties and utilizing in jazz more complex harmonies as demonstrated by Charles Ives and the traditional European contributions of Brahms and Debussy. Even though popular songs remained basically tonal, i.e. key oriented, the tendency was to add more sevenths. Thus, the beginning of jazz was again reflected in the earlier forms. Yet the simpler style of the old harmonies was never really completely abandoned for the newer ones.

As minstrelsy aged, personalities who distinguished themselves more as composers than performers were Hubert (Eubie) Blake, Robert Cole, Will Cook, H. T. Burleigh, and J. Rosamond Johnson. While many persons also wrote in art music styles, depending upon the circumstances and educational advantages, most composers like Fats Waller, W. C. Handy and Duke Ellington were almost always connected with jazz and similar forms. On the other hand, some like Burleigh ultimately became standard names in art songs and spirituals.

WILL MARION COOK (1869-1944)

Will Marion Cook, a native of Washington, D.C., was a talented musician of many styles. Educated at the Hochschule in Berlin, he later studied at Oberlin College and the National Conservatory of Music. A violinist of repute, he teamed with Bert Williams, William Moore, H. B. Smith, Cecil Mack, James Weldon Johnson, Alex Rogers and others to create some of the best musicals of that time. He also found the time to write classical and popular music, although his recognition was gained mostly through popular music.

Cook wrote tonal music consisting of ballads and the music of show business, as well as various arrangements of folk tunes and original compositions. His music was written for several types of instrumental and vocal forms. Among them were stage scores for *In Dahomey, Abyssinia* and *Banana Land; Springtime, Bon Bon Buddy, Creole Dance, Down de Lover's Lane, Exhortation* (Negro Sermon), *An Explanation, Fas' Fas' World, A Little Bit of Heaven Called Home, The Little Gypsy Maid, Love Is the Tend'rest of Themes, Manny, Red Red Rose, Sing Along, Mandy Lou, Mammy Lasses Candy Chile, On Emancipation Day, Rain Song, Until Then, Wid de Moon, Moon, Moon, Clorindy* and *Who Dat Say Chicken in This Crowd.*

JOHN ROSAMOND JOHNSON (1873-1954)

John Rosamond Johnson, brother of James Weldon, was born in Jacksonville, Florida. His wide range of experiences consisted of study at the University of Atlanta and the New England Conservatory with David Bispham. A pianist-singer, he toured America and. Europe in programs of spirituals, and in *Porgy and Bess.*

During the "Black Renaissance", Johnson teamed with both James Weldon Johnson and Robert Cole to produce a large quantity of highly popular songs used in musicals and variety shows. With his brother, he wrote the "Negro National Anthem," *Lift Ev'ry Voice and Sing,* as seen in Example 21 (see pages 58 and 59).

Other songs published with his brother were the *American Negro Spirituals, Rolling Along in Song,* a history of "Negro music" with 85 arrangements and a host of other songs for the minstrel and stage shows. Johnson also wrote: *African Drum Dance* (ballet), *I Told My Love to the Roses, Morning, Noon, and Night, Now Let Me Fly, O, Southland, Little Gal, Since You Went Away, I Ain't Going' Study War No More, Go Chain de Lion Down,* and *My Castle on the Nile.*

TIM J. BRYMN (1881-1946)

Tim J. Brymn, composer, conductor and arranger, was born in Kinston, North Carolina. Educated at Christian Institute, Shaw University and the National Conservatory of Music in New York City, he was well qualified to serve as music director of the Clef Club, and to function in the grand manner of the minstrel-jazz composers.

Brymn led the orchestra in Reisenweber's Jardin de Dance, Ziegfeld Roof and other places. During World War I, he served as the leader of the musical unit, 350 Field Artillery, AEF. Often using Chris Smith and Clarence Williams as collaborators, he wrote the following works: *Please Go Way and Let Me Sleep, La Rhumba, Shout, Sister, Shout, Josephine, My Joe, Camel Walk, Look Into Your Baby's Face and Say Goo-goo, My Pillow and Me,* and many others.

FORD DABNEY (1883-1958)

Ford Dabney, a Washingtonian who eventually settled in New York, was another composer engaged in the area of early jazz and minstrelsy. A member of ASCAP in 1937, he was educated at the Armstrong Manual Training School. He also studied with his father, Charles Dach, William Walddecker, Samuel Fabian and others. As the official court musician for the President of Haiti in 1904, Dabney was competent, but was not as publicized as other composers.

When Dabney returned to the United States in 1907, he led his own quartet, conducted the Ziegfeld Midnight Frolics orchestra for eight years, created the original dance numbers for the Vernon Castles, the famous dancers, and organized the Tempo Club, a Negro talent bureau. He participated in the musical activities of the day by writing for films, vaudeville theatres, composing and touring. Among his compositions were: *Porto Rico* (Rag Intermezzo), *Reach for the Ceiling, Rang Tang* (broadway stage score), *That Minor Strain, Oh You Devil* and *Shine.*

J. HUBERT (EUBIE) BLAKE (1883-   )

J. Hubert Blake, an early ragtime pianist-composer of reknown, is still active as a performer and composer. Born in Baltimore, Maryland, he later traveled to New York and became associated with the Harlem Renaissance while mainly developing a reputation as a composer of musicals. Blake has established himself as a writer of popular music, and according to recent television performances, still demonstrates ability at the piano.

Educated at New York University, Blake studied with Marshall Wil-

Lift Ev'ry Voice And Sing

Lyric by
JAMES WELDON JOHNSON
A. S. C. A. P.

Music by
J. ROSAMOND JOHNSON
A. S. C. A. P.

Ex. 21. *Lift Ev'ry Voice and Sing,* by J. Rosamond and James Weldon Johnson.
Copyright, Edward B. Marks Music Corporation. Used by permission.

Lib - er - ty; Let our re - joic - ing rise High as the
born____ had died; Yet with a stead - y beat, Have not our
on____ the way; Thou who hast by Thy might, Led us in -

list - 'ning____ skies, Let it re - sound loud as the roll - ing sea.____
wear - y____ feet Come to the place for which our fa - thers sighed?
to the light, Keep us for - ev - er in the path,____ we pray.____

poco meno mosso

Sing a song full of the faith that the dark past has taught us;
We have come o - ver a way that with tears has been wa - tered;
Lest our feet stray from the pla - ces, our God, where we met Thee,

mp poco meno mosso

son and others. While performing as pianist and organist at local cafes, vaudeville shows, and other places of entertainment, he later returned to his studies around 1950 as a student of the Schillinger method of composition. With Noble Sissle, he was a member of the vaudeville team which composed and performed the musicals *Shuffle Along* and *Chocolate Dandies*. Once the assistant conductor to Jim Europe of the Clef Club, he toured with the musical show organized by Europe for the United States Infantry. Recently, Blake was honored with other musicians at the New World Symphony Orchestra Dinner held on October 5, 1969, in New York. In addition to other lectures and concerts, he has also appeared on such television shows as David Frost and other talk shows.

Blake's list of works included the following: *Charleston Rag, You Were Meant for Me, Shuffle Along, Chocolate Dandies, Baby Mine, Love will Find a Way, Loving You the Way I Do, Memories of You, My Handy Man Ain't Handy Anymore, That Lindy Hop, You're Lucky to Me, Swanee Home, Roll Jordan, Tricky Fingers, Troublesome Ivories, Dictys on Seventh Avenue, Fizz Water* and *The Chevy Chase.*

Other Composers

The list of Black involvement in later minstrelsy is so long that it would not be practical to review it all. While some composers who practiced minstrelsy will also be discussed in early jazz, a considerable number of other Blacks connected with early music are excerpted in a list compiled by W. C. Handy in 1937: Cecil Mack, *Teasing;* Joe Trent, *Muddy Waters;* Maceo Pinkard, *Mammy O' Mine, Sweet Georgia Brown, Congratulations* and *Mammy;* J. C. Johnson, *Believe It, Beloved, Old Fashioned Love;* Will Vodery, *Tomorrow;* Henry Creamer, *Way Down Yonder in New Orleans* and *After You're Gone;* Porter Grainger, *Cotton;* Clarence Muse, *Sleepy Time Down South;* Perry Bradford, *Crazy Blues;* Peter Bocage, *Mama's Gone Goodbye;* Charles Warfield, *Baby, Won't You Please Come Home;* Spencer Williams, *Everybody Loves My Baby* and *I've Found a New Baby;* King Oliver, *Sugar Foot Stomp;* Bennie Benjamin, *I Don't Want to Set the World on Fire* and *When the Lights Go on Again All Over the World;* Shelton Brooks, *Some of These Days;* Lucky Roberts, *Moonlight Cocktail;* Ernest Hogan, *All Coons Look Alike to Me;* Al John, *Go Way Back and Sit Down;* and the Spikes Brothers and Benny Carter, *Some Day Sweetheart.*

The Influence of Black Minstrelsy

As in the case of other early Black music, the growth of minstrel songs paralleled Baroque, Classical and Romantic periods. While contemporary with some of the early Euro-American composers as Billings, Mason, Hopkinson, McDowell, Carpenter and Paine, minstrelsy was well aware of slave music.

As songs of the minstrel shows were developed with an intermingling of European and African developments transplanted to America, they, in

60

turn, influenced music being written in Europe. The dances influenced the music of Coleridge-Taylor (1875-1912), an Anglo-African. Claude Debussy (1862-1918) was a European composer who used elements of minstrelsy in his compositions, such as in Golliwog's *Cakewalk,* which made use of cake-walk dance rhythms — quick notes alternating with slow notes (♫♫ ♫). Another musician who was greatly influenced by such music was the concert pianist Louis Gottshalk (1829-1869). Born in New Orleans of French-Spanish or possibly Jewish-Creole ancestry, his fame was international. Songs heard during his childhood experiences were in his compositions *Banjo, Bamboula, Savane* and others, which used not only minstrel styles but African contributions as well. Gottshalk's constant association with these musical forms is recorded as practical historical information. Born before Dvorak, he was not given due credit for having pioneered indigenous music in quest of American nationalism.

As a total entity, the minstrel show also served as the basis for vaudeville, burlesque and other musicals of the tin pan variety. The instrumentation found in minstrelsy was vital in supplying gems for early jazz ensembles and in developing characteristic instrumental idioms used in all the popular forms. Fortunately, the offspring of minstrelsy fared better than the blackface era in bringing to the world an acceptance of its musical style and performance.

VII
JAZZ:
ITS DEFINITION, HISTORY AND INFLUENCE

Jazz has become the highest developed, most complicated music derived from mostly American folk sources. Jazz is intellectual, yet relaxed; classical yet popular; base yet lofty; delicate and hilarious. It primarily is an instrumental style, but has been strongly influenced vocally and includes many musical elements, timbres and moods. Neither sacred nor secular, its emotions have remained of the church and of the world.

Because the Afro-American has been most responsible for formation and its major developments, there is no doubt that jazz consists of the summation of the Black man's experience as well as a review of his culture. There is no music which encompasses more of Black lifestyle.

There is no other music which relates more of being American and of the relationships between various peoples. Its synthesis is a product of African and European influences, making jazz an all-inclusive form. Other forms are not readily adaptable to fit multiple occasions. Jazz is!

Definition

Jazz has been defined as improvisation, blues, ragtime, soul or rhythm. Perhaps stemming from "jazz," the sexual term from Creole patois applied to the Congo dances of New Orleans, the derivatives and synonyms also included "razz," meaning to "tease, ridicule or heckle." Jazz, razz, jass and rag, as well as jig and shout have long since been constituents and associated terms.

However, jazz was not only blues, or a shout, a jig or a clog. Yet it was greatly influenced by all of these elements, from the movement of a "shout" to the dotted manner of a jig. They were *of* jazz, but each alone was not jazz itself.

Nor was jazz just improvisation alone, as this would have denied the written melody, harmony and rhythm, and would have restricted jazz to a definition of spontaneity. Jazz was not just rhythm, although rhythm was the most characteristic aspect of Africanism and excitement. Also, rhythm was seemingly the most influential factor to influence other forms.

Jazz, then, was a collective term implying many features. In general, it was a combination of blues, ragtime, jubilee songs, shouts, jigs, clogs, coon songs and African-American primitivism, i.e., old, ancient or early, and not crude or "uncivilized." This collection utilized both secular and religious forms, including idioms of both popular and classical music.

62

Specifically, jazz was also a verb, meaning to improvise by additions of tones or by the dotting of rhythms. And like the definition of African music, jazz was a correlation of speech with music and dance, wherein instruments "spoke" the sounds of an intense melody while inspiring the listeners to partake by a responsive motion.

Jazz was to folk music what a fugue was to art music. And like a fugue, its principles could be incorporated into any musical style. Jazz techniques referred to a method of practice. As a technique which had collective forms, and like a fugue, it was the culmination of previous forms. To some, jazz eventually became the "classical music of the Blacks" because of its origins and its ultimate accomplishment as an art form, and even more so because European-based art music also began from similar origins of popularism (see Chapter XV).

Jazz originally differed from art music in its function. Although jazz partially flourished in church, its main purpose was for dance and entertainment, and not for intellectual consideration. Black musicians of the Awakening Period were not allowed free access to either ballrooms, clubs or concert halls. Therefore, jazz was relegated to cheap dance halls and the like. Partly because of unfair unions, segregation and "Jim Crow" laws, and partly because Whites in art music felt that Blacks were inferior in mind and in mastering a skill, jazz was further distinguished by the fact that its audience was mainly Black. Blacks bought blues recordings, enjoyed jazz in the clubs and cafes, and developed their own rules for participation. Its popularity, financial possibilities and excitement eventually attracted Whites.

Most significantly, jazz further differentiated itself from traditional art music and most smaller popular forms in that it made use of changing harmonies such as the constant sevenths in one period and a mixture of sevenths with altered chords from the mid-1900's onward. Other forms used triads (chords with three notes) while using sevenths, ninths and altered chords less frequently. In addition, jazz rhythm was one of its more characteristic aspects with its daring syncopations and cross rhythms not as commonly noted in art music.

History

The birthplace of jazz is speculative. At first, historians and the publishing media ignored the art and delegated the responsibility of its promotion mainly to chance. Because similar musical activities began in Kansas, St. Louis, Chicago, New Orleans and New York, it is inaccurate to say that the center of greatest activity was developed in New Orleans, or that New Orleans was the birthplace of jazz. The eighty-five-year-old musician, Eubie Blake, has indicated that he heard jazz in New York when only a child and we should remember that Duke Ellington heard jazz in Washington. Jazz participants included trained musicians who performed in classical and popular orchestras, musicians who played in the churches and streets and the appreciatively accompanying rhythms and shouts of the dancers. Original instruments were most often homemade or of modern western origin, depending on availability.

Jazz was publicized in the media around 1900. But the popularity of jazz and its origins must be distinguished. Its popularity reached a peak in the 1900's and drew the attention of more of the total populace than ever before. Speculation has since arisen concerning the originators of the name "jazz"; none is conclusive. Unlike the spirituals, the name just happened and no one could say who was responsible. Interviews printed by Rudi Blesh in *They All Played Ragtime* indicated that Blacks themselves named the music before newspapers began to use the term. Jelly Roll Morton also claimed to have originated the term "jazz," in spite of the work of his immediate predecessors.

As to the origin, Samuel Charters published *Jazz: New Orleans* in which he presented letters speculating on the subject. In some 1919 editions of the New York Dramatic Mirror, they stated that any of the following legends might have been responsible for the name:

1. Bert Kelly and his "Jas" Comedy Band";
2. A boy from New Orleans, "Stalebread," and his "Spasm Band";
3. The jazz effects of "Right at Em's Razz Band"; or
4. The various names of the "Negro" orchestras of New Orleans who played at picnics, outings and funerals.

Through evolutionary stages, jazz must surely be older than eighty years. Its origins in blues, spirituals, ballads, coon songs, shouts, jigs and rags were performed long before the title of jazz was given. The forms were definitely perpetuated within minstrel shows and similar places and the religious and secular emotions had long since been a part of the music of minstrelsy, from whose bands jazz was partly derived.

For a long time, there have been diverse opinions about the exact historical periods of jazz, an argument not easily resolved and certainly not intended to be solved here. Yet it is important to know that in *Jazz: Its Evolution and Essence,* Hodeir categorized jazz into several sections: Primitive (beginning at approximately 1900); Oldtime, Pre-Classical, Classical and Modern, (the latter beginning in 1945). In the *Harvard Dictionary* of *Music,* Willi Apel divided the periods into some five discussions covering stylistic trends of ragtime in 1890, blues, jazz, hot jazz, sweet, boogie (and contrapuntal types, etc.); swing from 1935, and modern. John Mehegan designated 1875 as the beginning of an Archaic period. Tanner and Gerow in their *Jazz,* traced European and African heritages while indicating periodic styles and techniques of basic blues (although they unfortunately do not use blues in the chronological development of jazz). They also typed jazz from dixieland to third stream. The untidiness of the many lists, and the lack of conformity in describing eras, together with the disagreement of dates, stem both from differences in interpretation as well as the personal stresses of information available.

Jazz did not begin suddenly in 1880 if we depend upon the foregoing discussions and include the opinions of musicians and letters of documentation. Its advances were evolutionary. Therefore, the "archaic," "primitive" or ancient origins of jazz should probably cover the earliest roots developed in slavery and minstrelsy. Using African inheritance as the primary source, this first era would overlap with that of minstrelsy and early folk forms, for those minstrels before 1830 used those folk forms and continued to do so after the Civil War. For example, W. C. Handy and Willie (the Lion) Smith related to Leonard Feather the same facts as Eubie Blake. They stated that the music which they heard as children was the same jazz which they improved upon later. The "jazzy" strains of Louis Gottshalk also indicated that he must have heard similar music which influenced him some forty years before Handy and Smith were born.

The second stage of jazz, then, could well begin around Reconstruction when many more Black professionals emerged on stage as performers in their own right, and performed that which they had both heard and practiced themselves. This would be the era of Handy and Smith, George Milburn, James Bland, and Sam Lucas, the latter three of whom were already involved in composing and performing the minstrel-style music which was to directly influence the performance and compositional aspects of jazz. Eventually others began emphasizing jigs, clogs, shouts, blues, coon songs and ragtime.

By early 1900, a third stage began whose era of achievements and personalities included Louis Armstrong, Duke Ellington, the Johnsons, the Smiths and older musicians who molded jazz into an independent and recognized art form. They practiced dixieland blues and swing styles while continuing to improve upon the rags and other smaller forms.

The span of the 1940's and 1950's saw Charlie Parker, Lionel Hampton, Thelonius Monk, Coleman Hawkins and others who made significant changes in melodic, harmonic and other elemental structures, and who further developed jazz into a more sophisticated type of music. Some of the dance characteristics subsided and gave way to faster tempos and challenging timbres and techniques. However, the 1950's introduced cool, progressive and other modern styles which revolted against the trends of tempos and literal loquaciousness of bop and other forms, while retaining the difficulty of form, timbres and harmonic concepts.

The Influence of Jazz

Once a totally Black involvement, jazz developed a reputation for being loud, bawdy, untamed and low-class. Yet Jazz influenced orchestrations, harmonic outlines, rhythms, forms and titles of both European and American music. Its polyrhythmic, improvisational and constantly syncopated elements also filtered into "chance music" as well as art music and other popular tin pan forms. From the use of the saxophone, the banjo, the expanded ranges and techniques found in some classical symphonic compositions to the characteristic emotions, melodies and harmonies, jazz influenced greatly. Itself influenced by classical music, jazz has reciprocated, encountered, reacted and emerged into a body of sound almost indistinguishable from art music. Some composers of many nationalities who were directly or indirectly influenced by jazz are listed below. As further

65

proof of the jazz influence, Aaron Copland's book, *New Music,* directly shows the scope of this fact during the entire modern period by illustrating certain compositions where jazz is contained and by including himself as one of those influenced by jazz.

Composers and Compositions Influenced by Jazz Elements

Bernstein, Leonard (1918-)	*Mass; West Side Story; Concerto for Piano*
Gottshalk, Louis (1829-1869)	*Banjo; Bamboula*
Satie, Erik (1866-1925)	Parade (ballet *Ragtime du Paquebot*)
Ravel, Maurice (1875-1937)	*Violin Sonata; Piano Concerto in G*
Stravinsky, Igor (1882-1971)	*Histoire du Soldat; Piano Rag Music; Ragtime for Eleven Instruments*
Milhaud, Darius (1892-)	*Scaramouche; La Creation du Monde*
Still, William Grant (1895-)	*Afro-American Symphony*
Gershwin, George (1898-1937)	*Rhapsody in Blue; Porgy and Bess; Three Preludes; Concerto in F*
Chavez, Carlos (1899-)	*Fox Blues*
Copland, Aaron (1900-)	*Concerto* for piano and orchestra
Krenek, Ernst (1900-)	*Johnny Spielt Auf*
Weill, Kurt (1900-1950)	*Three Penny Opera*
Work, John III (1901-1967)	*Sassafras; Appalachia*
Bonds, Margaret (1913-1972)	*I Got a Home In-a That Rock*
Carter, John (1937-)	*Cantata*

VIII
JAZZ FORMS, STYLES, TECHNIQUES AND PERFORMANCE

Although based on similar modes of emotional and formal construction, jazz forms have not always been as easy to define as art music forms. For whereas classical theorists had formulated rules for fugues, sonatas and symphonies long before jazz was published and popularized, no one in early jazz bothered to establish such rules, and few cared to do so. Those who wished to organize it into a formally "accepted" art were countered by others who gloried in its absolute freedom of movement within structures.

Nevertheless, a most important substance of jazz was its form, i.e., its total collection of outlines, plans or organized formulas. Since any melody or pattern had shape, jazz structure or improvisational figures contained form, either well planned and distinctly scored and materialized by chance and personal taste during "jam sessions" and free improvisations, or being formulated from all structures which contributed to the overall development of jazz.

Traditionally, jazz has been defined as a rhythmic or improvisatory technique, a fact suggesting that jazz was a way of playing, rather than a kind of piece. Most decidedly, jazz was indeed a way of playing within improvisations of rhythms and harmonic contexts, but it also entailed form. Just as historians were never satisfied with the answer that problematic liturgical chants contained merely "free rhythm", so should scholars not be content with the treacherous simplicity of a statement that jazz implied no form. It is important, however, that the term "jazz" implied not one, but a collection of forms. (see Chapter VII). The idea of form in jazz, then, was its end product — that is, its collection of traditional forms, hybrids and arrangements, as well as its original structures.

The earliest of these consisted of those pieces influenced by traditional calls, hollers, spirituals, blues, work songs and hybrid art music compositions of vocal and instrumental types. Later forms were influenced by marches, preludes, ballads, ternary and binary structures, rhapsodic or fantasy-like pieces, quadrilles, fugues and toccatas. The contemporary era has already witnessed more extended varieties from jazz ballet, operas and symphonies to liturgical masses.

While early jazz sprang from African outgrowths which were directly influenced by the oral tradition, still other aspects of jazz were inherited from European art music. Numerical systems for measures of entire pieces

67

and phrases were borrowed from European standards consisting of eight, twelve or sixteen bars, or symmetry in general. European contributions of harmony also served as the structural basis of more sophisticated forms along with melodic contours. Dependence upon textual outlines evolved also from Africa such as the call and response, improvisation and other formal elements.

The foregoing chapter has presented the general history of jazz by outlining some of its definitions and generalities about the music. Mostly multifunctional, these musical contributions are now discussed as interchangeable relationships within several formal contexts. Some important forms, styles and techniques are introduced in some detail below, based on the characteristic styles of the composers from the late 1800's to the 1950's.

Ragtime

Emerging from minstrel bands, ragtime was popularized in the late 1800's. It was born earlier than the first published composition by the Black composer, Thomas Turpin, whose *Harlem Rag* was succeeded by many others like Scott Joplin, Jelly Roll Morton, Louis Chauvin, James Scott, Anthony Jackson, Luckey Roberts, James P. Johnson, Bob Caldwell and Fats Waller.

Although having been influenced by singers, bands, banjo and other instruments, the pianist became a preferred substitute for familiar minstrel ensembles at clubs and cabarets. Primarily because of economics, this caused the piano to ultimately dominate ragtime at one time. Yet it was clear that the piano style became unique only after its associations with the "missing" instruments which it imitated.

At one time, ragtime could have been synonymous with the music called jazz. Rudi Blesh stated that "Negro ragtime was essentially an instance of racial improvisation" while H. E. Krehbiel, in the preface of his *Afro-American Folksongs,* felt that rag was a debased form of the spiritual. Some others referred to rag as "clogging," "shuffling" or "swinging," all terms of which partly defined certain aspects of minstrelsy as well as jazz. Besides the elements of improvisation, ragtime was also composed music, much of which was written and performed by outstanding Black musicians.

Ragtime was both classically and popularly oriented. Some composers of the form termed it "classical" music. Not only was it influenced by the styles of the nineteenth century concepts of the quadrilles, marches and other solo pieces, but also by the coon songs, shouts, clogs, jigs, ballads, banjo pieces, country dances and so-called "barrelhouse rhythms" of the Blacks. Ragtime was often a multi-sectional composition, representative of many piano solo pieces of the nineteenth century.

Ragtime was technically difficult, and consisted of eighth note or sixteenth note figurations above a walking, "um pah" bass, whose main beats and frames were quite march-like. Its rhythm was frequently that of the "cake-walk" (♪♪♪). Generally, the melody was syncopated or dotted

68

and was ornamented above a bass which jumped about from register to register. Sometimes the bass made use of double octaves or single tones in sounding the root on the first and third beats, and alternated with the other chord tones on the second and fourth beats. Another feature of the bass line was the inclusion of the tenth with the root and third or fifth of the chord being played simultaneously with one hand. Still other examples, as in the music of Joplin and James Johnson, resembled "etudes" or studies similar to art music examples of the nineteenth century, particularly the A and E Minor *Etudes* of Frederick Chopin, as compared in Examples 22 and 23:

Ex. 22. Ragtime techniques.

Etudes in A and E Minor, Opus 25, Nos. 4 and 5, Chopin.

The "walking" characteristic found in ragtime involved a manner of accenting the offbeat of the bass pattern. Most often written in duple time, this was referred to as "stride" piano. It involved mainly diatonic movement in the left hand, and often was accompanied by foot stamping. In his *Ragtime Instruction Book,* Joplin instructed that rags were not to be played at a fast tempo. Discussions of tempo by other composers instructed one to play either fast or slow. Since "stride" implied a walking gait, the term necessarily depended upon whoever did the "walking" and therefore left a problem as to approximate tempos. However, stride did resemble a proud, show-off manner of performance, thus perhaps implying a maestoso movement, as illustrated in Example 23.

Ex. 23. Walking basses

69

In addition to being played by small band ensembles or piano, ragtime music was also sung, particularly as in minstrel and vaudeville ballads. *Ragtime Songbooks* listed a vocal version of Scott Joplin's *Maple Leaf Rag* in comic lyrics, shown in Example 24, which makes use of the same theme as in the piano version of Example 31.

Ex. 24. *Maple Leaf Rag,* vocal version, Joplin. © Copyright, Edward B. Marks Music Corporation. Used by permission.

Blues

Perhaps the blues has influenced jazz more than any other form. So great has been this association that the very soul of jazz has been primarily defined around it, sometimes under the guise of "soul music". When W. C. Handy published his *Memphis Blues* and his *Saint Louis Blues,* the blues gained unexpected publicity which highlighted and promoted it to a position above that which had not been seen for decades in the minstrel shows. Although some writers have not realized the blues as part of jazz history, there is no question as to the validity of blues within the framework of such jazz bands or jazz *per se.*

Virtually a vocal form, the blues was born years before the birth of Handy, and was derived from the same emotional and environmental experiences as those which produced the work songs, spirituals, calls and hollers. Its popularity, however, did not occur until around 1915, somewhat overshadowing the craze for ragtime. The blues has never yet released its effect of melodic, harmonic and emotional concepts from the entities of jazz styles.

Generally secular, the words were important to the blues. Into the blues went both the religious and secular moods of Blacks. For as a man felt, he played and composed. Ecstatic emotions of the church gleaned from the belief in a Deliverer were coupled with the bewilderment of a lost love. Topical developments ranged from the time of day to the position of an individual in society. And politics, segregation, housing, WPA and the depression were pitted against the accompaniment of musical prayers exhibited in up-tempo "blue jazz" processions for funerals.

It is interesting to note that recorded evidence strongly resembling both gospel and jazz fused with blues elements have been collected from various church services by Lomax, Spivacke and others. Their performances, instrumentations and emotions bordered on the secular forms. Some of these examples were entitled *Wasn't That a Mighty Storm, Certainly, Lord, Oh, The Lamb of God, The Lord Done Sanctified Me* and *Do Lord, Remember Me.* The fact could not be ignored that some of the blues and jazz sessions were about as "sanctified" in spirit as were these religious songs, and that the religious songs, when slow, were just as "bluesy" as the blues.

Exceptions to the contrary, standard blues form usually consisted of twelve measures, having three lines of poetry whose first and second lines were identical. An illustration of both the "classic" structure and the poetic form are shown in Example 25.

Ex. 25. 12-bar blues with melodic outline and poetic scheme.

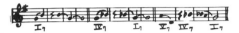

Woke up dis mawning, found m' baby gone,
Woke up dis mawning, found m' baby gone,
If she went to stay, I won't be here too long.

A great variety of blues forms consisted of two-part, three-part, or small through-composed forms. Some blues contained as many as 32 measures, or as few as eight. Ballads, spiritual and strophic forms were also used.

The blues made use of "blue notes," so named to denote sad or mournful qualities and were chromatic-like or semi-tone waverings between major and minor thirds, or simply the lowering of the third and seventh of a scale. Mainly derived from African scales and vocal approximations of tones, this was a natural characteristic inherent in the language and the ornamented melodic lines.

Blues melodies served as the focal point of interest, but also suggested the harmonic punctuations of the accompaniment. Most often of a homophonic or chordal texture, the form made use of tonal chord progressions in support of generally small melodic intervals, occasionally interspersed with larger skips of sevenths, fourths, fifths and octaves. The commonest progressions were I, IV, I, V, I or later, 17, IV7, V7, IV7, 17. As in the case of many Afro-American songs, the blues showed a strong preference for thirds, particularly in the cadential or ending patterns. Some of the musical characteristics discussed here are shown in Example 26.

Ex. 26. Blues progressions, harmonic, melodic, cadential.

a. simple chords
b. complex chords
c. melodic idioms
d. cadential patterns

71

The new "rhythm and blues" pointed out the importance of the musical element of movement with emotion, a closer harmonic base to jazz complexities and more instrumental qualities. Next to the text, all blues forms revealed the nature of spontaneous rhythm from a spoken language. Not altogether as simple as its verse, however, blues rhythms were composed in long notes such as whole, halves, quarters and eighths, which in actual performance, were intended to be improvised into shorter ornamental note values. Triplets, mixtures of rests in elongated or syncopated fashion, sixteenths and thirty-second notes were also sparingly used, except in ornamentation. Although most blues appeared in duple meter and also retained the same meter throughout, rare cases of frequently changing meters within the short tunes were used. The following chart shows some of the rhythmic practices of blues which were ultimately used and rejuvenated by jazz performers and composers.

Ex. 27. Chart of blues rhythms.

Boogie-Woogie

Around 1930, ragtime was supplanted by still another piano style, the boogie-woogie. A rowdy, fun-type composition, the boogie seemed unrelated to the heartfelt emotions of the blues or the whines of calls and hollers. It rather lent itself to a complete abandonment of the weariness of foregoing centuries and encouraged an optimistic anticipation of newer things, and more advanced opportunities growing out of the era of the depression and of the "Black Renaissance."

Partly derived from guitar principles as well as other instrumental timbres, boogie was sometimes used in vocal ballads as accompaniment figures or as a spontaneous technique to excite one to dance the "hucklebuck" or the "jitterbug." Beside the ballad-type structure, there were original, through-composed compositions and some in ternary form. Boogie-woogie forms further consisted of "ostinato" principles which were repeated short bass figurations of eight eighth notes per measure.

The "jumping" or "bouncing" quality of boogie rhythms was conceived by simply dotting the bass notes, as in ragtime, or by using jagged rhythms in the melody as well. Even when the score did not indicate the dotted effects, it was expected in the actual performance. Written in duple time, boogie concentrated its efforts upon an ornamental melody above swiftly moving progressions of tonic, sub-dominant and tonic (I, IV, I, V, I or I, IV, V7, I), usually with an addition of seventh tones.

Technically, boogie basses were not too unlike some octaves, tremolos and arpeggios used in Beethoven or Mozart sonatas. It was also similar to ragtime techniques. Yet the rotating sound of the boogie was far more comprehensible and manageable than either the bass of ragtime or the sonatas of the Classical composers. The most common of boogie patterns are shown in Example 28; they were either alternated within sections, or one pattern was continued throughout the composition.

Ex. 28. Boogie patterns.

Gospel

Gospel music, a vocal form used mainly for church worship but also found in night clubs and concert halls, originated before its popularity in the 1920's. Although more often a technique than an original form, gospels were nevertheless products interwoven with the forms of the blues, spirituals and the frenzied shout. Gospels differed from spirituals in that they did not bear the simplicity of style of the older songs. They were not used as protest or survival songs and were directed toward revelation, evangelical teachings, revivalism and good will. They stressed the "coming of the Lord" and were not sung with ambiguity or allegory. A happy spirit and one's general worth were intentionally stressed.

Like the blues, the most important characteristic of gospel music was the word communication. Deriving its messages from late Biblical (New Testament) or original sources, either narrative or ornamental techniques of the blues and folk songs were common. The use of word interpolations between lines such as "ummn," "Lord," "oh," "yes" and other phrases was typical. Unquestionably, words determined the ultimate style of the melodic line and their meaning would direct the corresponding rise and fall of the pitches. Directly related to the words, the element of emotion was next in importance to these songs which sought to save the soul.

Tambourines, guitars, trombones, clarinets, organs and pianos were generally most frequently used as accompanying media when the compositions were not performed in "a cappella" fashion. Clapping, an African concept of drumming, also accompanied the voices. Harmonically, gospels were tonal, and were not much influenced by atonal harmonies of the 1900's. By 1960, however, general jazz chords employed almost constant seventh and ninth intervals. Some pieces often paralleled the harmonies and styles of rock.

Rhythmically, jazz penetrated gospel in syncopated techniques, accents and complex polyphony. The use of obligatos assisted in the rhythmic polyphony. Basically, however, gospel was homophonic. Some of the most characteristic techniques have included dotted notes and frequent instrumental "breaks." Whether or not gospel was simply the name for church or liturgical jazz, the subject became one of conflict mainly because of its rhythmic factors which inspired close similarity to rhythms of shouts as well as other dances. The interpolation of chords and arpeggios became standard means by which triplet figures or sixteenths and eighths against the quarter caused the dance-like spirit as shown in Example 29.

Ex. 29. Gospel techniques (rhythmic and melodic).

a. Original hymn tune
b. Gospel improvisation

Rock

Rock and Roll was a later outgrowth of jazz. Designed primarily for dance, its popularity became real during the early 1950's. Greatly influenced by the boogie-woogie and blues, it settled into the style and presentation of gospel music. Like gospel, the most important aspect of rock was the message and the emotion of high-pitched sounds and loud dynamics. Based on secular subjects, rock expanded and capitalized upon interpolation, fragments and additions to lines of poetry such as in gospel. Entire structures could be based upon expansions of words such as "Oh Yeah," "Babeeee," "Uh" and "Uh Huh," sung in either a fluid melismatic style or in a hollering production.

The harmony of rock emphasized the tonic and subdominant chords, and generally terminated with the plagal cadence of IV to I, or it could follow the standard classical pattern of I, IV, V, I. In general, these harmonic trends were the same as in gospels.

Before the popularity of Aretha Franklin and Jim Hendrix, rock was more monotonous than gospel music, and less imaginative. Originally for dance, it has now grown to include music for listening, and the sounds of the electronic and space age have furthermore rendered the form more interesting. Once commonly performed as a vocal group or soloist with a small rhythm section of drums, piano and guitar, the media has now expanded into using more woodwinds and brass, or (as in the case of Joe Creech) strings.

The form of rock was built around ballads or tin pan forms. Like the gospels, it also resembled the blues in its waverings of pitch with short sections, or within strophic or free-style forms. The use of instruments, in addition to accompanying the voice, also expanded the form with short introductions or by engaging in "breaks" or interludes during the progress of the songs.

Gospels, rock, blues, boogie, and ragtime have defined many forms, styles and trends which culminate in jazz. Themselves complete entities, they have nevertheless formed a union of relative kinship to formulate the principles of great variety and similarity within jazz history.

Styles and Techniques

Style, a characteristic way of writing or performing music, was interrelated with technique, a mastery of the overall skills practiced in various types of jazz performance and composition. Thus, style and technique involved a method of procedure as well as a manipulation of idioms. In addition to forms, the history of jazz also represented evolutionary styles and techniques of respective composers as well as a tradition of performance bound by the emotions of each. Since musical developments in the past have always come as a kind of revolt against the emotions, styles and techniques of the preceding generation, the philosophy and practice of jazz musicians were not exceptions to this rule.

Many of the jazz idioms were difficult and varied enough to indicate concepts of subjective performance. Some of the most common of these styles could apply to more than one kind of music, and their terms implied as much emotion as form. For example, "sweet," "hot," "funky" and "cool" were descriptive words meaning pleasantness, improvisation and earthy activity, and the relaxed, subdued dynamics or emotions, respectively. These were aspects of style which could be determined by actually playing in a certain way and had to be considered in the following not only as forms, but as emotions.

"Dixieland" was developed between the 1890's and the 1900's, and may or may not have been chiefly the result of White achievement. Directly related to ragtime, it influenced most styles within the era of ragtime and blues, until it was replaced by the Chicago type around 1920. Based on individualism and melodic concepts, it resembled counterpoint of the Baroque period in its overall effects, but was a tonal example of band ensemble in jazz action. Besides its melodic make-up, timbre was important

75

to the sound of dixieland, whose early instrumentation consisted of a lead clarinet, a melodic cornet or trumpet and the trombone, tuba, banjo and drum. In Chicago, the piano and saxophone were added, and the guitar replaced the banjo. Particularly in dixieland, the clarinet served as one of the melody instruments whose rule it was to play eighth notes around the harmonies of the other instruments. The structure eventually sponsored ensemble playing against solo improvisations, but the outlines of the works were written out for the players to follow.

"Hot jazz" consisted of an exciting, energetic style of freedom to interpolate, to manipulate and to improvise. Made famous in the early 1920's, Louis Armstrong and others practiced the art. Hot jazz simplified harmonies, made use of "scat singing" or nonsense syllables, vibrato, piercing tones, high-pitched cadences and interrelated vocal aspects with those of instrumental ones. Although bands were directly involved with the style, the "hotness" of the era also penetrated piano and vocal styles, as well as categories of instruments dominated by the trumpet.

"Swing" was a term which defined motion for the set undertaking of big bands made popular during the 1920's. Its organization was larger than previous band ensembles, and it emphasized sections rather than single instruments; however, some solos were planned against a section. Generally, swing included brasses, woodwinds and percussion, the latter section of which consisted of the drums with piano, string bass and other varieties such as the vibraharp. Primarily designed for dances, swing was meant for the accompaniment of the two-step and other popular dances of the "charleston" days, and was usually composed in steady, duple time.

"Bebop" was a less intense emotion of popular form which was developed during the 1940's and extended into the 1950's. With the efforts of Charlie Parker and Dizzy Gillespie, followed by Thelonius Monk, Charlie Christian, Bud Powell and others, there began an emphasis upon improvisation, technique and faster tempos. Bop was characterized by the use of nonsensical language such as "Hey Boppa Rebop," being sung to the accompaniment of instruments, but used as either rhythm or expressions of joy. Accompanying accessories to the music were the unusual clothes worn. Dark shades, berets and short beards were common to the "hip," "knowledgeable" and "sharp" kind of music that was bop.

Bop was instrumental in returning to the melodic emphasis of instruments, instead of continuing the sectional and large ensembles of swing and was also more economical. It was also important to the preparation of more complex harmonies such as elevenths, thirteenths and dissonances in general. The ultimate aims directed themselves toward more difficult "classical" concepts of higher forms so to impress and inspire a listening audience to dwell on things intellectual.

After 1940, jazz became more polished, developed, difficult, and of greater variety than its predecessors. Greater independence of form and technique were established while retaining some basic characteristics of its

76

origins. Whereas similar motion had governed many of the older forms, varieties of devices such as contrary motion, polyphony and obligatos were now employed. Other features were extensions of melodic ranges and unisons. Instrumental styles promoted expanded registers; broken octaves transferred to melodic elements, with more grace notes, more solo emphasis, closer chord clusters, block chords and unique endings. Independence of parts and of inner voices were developed which were compelled to last longer than any time before, and with breathless urgency, jazz grew into a most complicated art form.

Performance

Performance involved a reconstructing of the music and an enlivening of the printed intentions of the composer. Therefore, all of the skills of jazz from ornamentation, basic progressions and even to the methods of decorum had to be perfected in order to begin, to sustain the interest of listeners and to terminate in a proper jazz style.

The best performer was one who was aware of the materials which a composer had at his disposal such as melody, harmony, etc. He was aware of their function, texture, balance and emotion. He concerned himself with improvisational skills, the reading of scores and a knowledge of composition.

Each successive era created greater demands on performance. Consequently, the best performers met the challenge by a ready knowledge of score reading, improvising written and unwritten music and developing instrumental or vocal skills as demanded by the musical materials. Amazingly, some Black performers developed fantastic skills without much formal study. Others, however, found that both the music and the competition were soon so strong that it was wiser to depend less on talent alone. Many of these performers became scholars of composition and have distinguished themselves as composers.

Of all the aspects of jazz, its rhythm was the most exciting and perhaps the most difficult of all of the elements to perform. One therefore had to be keenly aware and responsive to rhythmic alterations of dotting, augmenting and diminishing. It was the responsibility of the performer to practice all of the perfections in rhythm such as polymeters and polyrhythms. At first in duple time, jazz later included other meters, and by the era of cool and progressive, used multimeters or polymeters in rapid exchange.

Improvisation was the next most difficult feat to develop, since this required a knowledge of chords, scales, melodic direction and imagination. Symbols and other developments in art music from the Classical period to that of Charles Ives and Igor Stravinsky of the modern period influenced labels in jazz. Some others were defined differently. The varieties of chords, although derived from the same bass outlines and inversions, were depicted in many of the progressions shown in Example 30.

77

Ex. 30. Jazz techniques in performance.

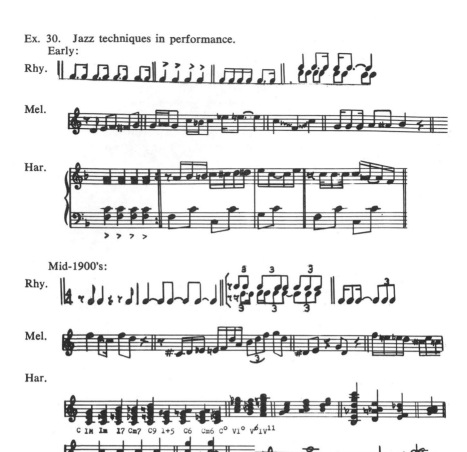

Code: M = major; m = minor; O — diminished; O = half-diminished;
       + = augmented

IX
JAZZ COMPOSERS

Complete documents of the earliest jazz performers and composers were not recorded in written history since many were found in plantation performances, minstrel shows, dance halls, outings and churches. Likewise, much of their music was performed but not necessarily written down. Although some musical types were somewhat parallel with recorded examples by the earliest White composers, most others could not have been exactly the same if we are to rely on the tradition of oral forms.

Blacks in early jazz and minstrelsy numbered quite a few. In part, they were Richard Milburn, William Turk, Sammy Ewell, (One-Leg) Willie Joseph, Jack The Bear, William Tyers, Blind Boone, Richard McLean, Plunk Henry and others. Some were born in the late 1800's or early 1900's. These were Thomas Turpin, Bob Caldwell, Stephen (Beetle) Henderson, (Piano) Price Davis, Tony Jackson, Sammy Davis, Jelly Roll Morton, Scott Joplin, Scott Hayden, Luckey Roberts, Arthur Marshall, James Scott and Louis Chauvin. Their successors were Willie (the Lion) Smith, Eubie Blake, James P. Johnson, Fats Waller, James Sylvester, Clarence Williams, and Fletcher Henderson. Only a few are represented here.

THOMAS M. TURPIN (1873-1922)

A significant pioneer who both influenced and inspired others to optimistic careers was Thomas M. Turpin. Born in Atlanta, Georgia, after the Civil War, he later moved to Saint Louis, Missouri, where he indulged in politics as well as music. Turpin was important because he was not only a competent composer, but was the first to publish a ragtime composition, *Harlem Rag,* which began the promotion and craze of the early jazz form. Published in 1897, it was succeeded by his *Bowery Buck, Ragtime Nightmare, St. Louis Rag, Buffalo, Siwash-Indian Rag, Pan-Am Rag,* and *When Sambo Goes to France.*

SCOTT JOPLIN (1868-1917)

Scott Joplin, around whose dates ragtime flourished, was the most outstanding composer, conductor and rag pianist of the late 1800's. Born in Texarkana, Texas, he lived in Sedalia, Missouri, before traveling to Saint Louis, Chicago and New York. As the teacher of Scott Hayden and Arthur Marshall, he was largely self-taught. He received lessons in piano, harmony and sight-reading from a local musician. It is doubtful that he studied

Fig. 7. Scott Joplin. Courtesy of Fisk University Library.

with Chauvin (1880-1908), except in a reciprocal association, as some sources seem to indicate. Chauvin and Joplin definitely collaborated in Saint Louis, where they both served as pianists at cafes, clubs and other places. Joplin also conducted the St. Louis World's Fair Orchestra in 1893, and was generally rated above the other local composers.

Recently, a revival of ragtime was made possible through the discoveries of his works, one of which was the opera *Treemonisha,* which enjoyed a premier performance in Atlanta, Georgia (with T. J. Anderson as the orchestrator). This staging was quickly followed by a programming of the same work at the Wolftrap Center in Washington, D.C.

Sometimes called the "Apostle of rag" or "Rag King," Joplin produced more than fifty rags and light classics, many of which were published, and some of which were given to the Fisk University Library to be microfilmed and catalogued in the Special Collections Room. Like Tom

Turpin, Luckey Roberts, Blind Boone, Eubie Blake and others, he felt that some of the ragtime music was classical and of European style. But his music was not as readily accepted in art music as were Gershwin's *Three Preludes,* Debussy's *Golliwog's Cakewalk* or examples by other White composers whose positions in society allowed them easy accessibility into professional musical circles. Some of Joplin's pieces resembled country dances, waltzes and pieces common to art music. Yet the consistent syncopations, dotted notes and "buck and wing" dance styles offered somewhat less variety than many of those by the above European composers. Nevertheless some of his compositions employed the same concepts as classical etudes or studies (Example 24), and as seen in his *Ragtime Instruction Book,* were equally difficult to perform. In his efforts to command respectability for his music, he objected to some of the "scat singing" and dirty word contexts of some rags.

One of the most famous of his piano rags was the *Maple Leaf Rag* in Ab major (Example 31, first sixteen bars). Structured into five sections with an emphasis upon the sub-dominant key in the fourth section, the work makes use of 2/4 meter, sixteenth note figurations of the right hand with sporadic chords being superimposed over a bass line of four eighth notes comprised of octaves and chords in alternation.

Ex. 31.   *Maple Leaf Rag,* Joplin. Copyright Edward B. Marks Music Corporation. Used by permission.

Some of Joplin's works were: *Sunflower Rag, School of Ragtime, Maple Leaf Rag, Palm Leaf Rag, Euphonic Sounds, Pineapple Rag, Sugar Cane Rag, Country Club Rag, Wall Street Rag, Pleasant Moments, Solace, Frolic of the Bars, Kismet Rag, Entertainer Rag, Original Rag, Treemonisha, Magnetic Rag, Hilarity Rag, Frogs Leg Rag, A Picture of Her Face* (waltz), *Please Say You Will, Mississippi Rag, The Great Crush Collision March, Combination March, Harmony Waltz, Swipsy Cakewalk, Sunflower Slow Drag, Peacherine Rag, The Easy Winners, Augustan Club Waltzes, I'm Thinking of My Pickanniny Days, A Breeze From Alabama, Cleopha Two-Step, March Majestic, Ragtime Dance, Elite Syncopations, The Entertainer, A Guest of Honor, The Strenuous Life, Weeping Willow, Something Doing, Little Black Boy, The Cascades, Heliotrope Bouquet* and *Stoptime Rag.*

WILLIAM CHRISTOPHER HANDY (1873-1958)

William C. Handy was born shortly after Scott Joplin, but earned his fame as "Father of the Blues" when he became the first publisher of written blues. Born in Florence, Alabama, he later settled in Memphis, Tennessee, where he was a band director, composer and performer. Even though Handy was a teacher, his education was mostly gained in the public schools. He nevertheless became one of the giants in the field of popular music, and his talents were recognized for his arrangements of music from jazz to Black spirituals.

During his career, Handy became a member of NAACC, led the Mahara Minstrels, made various recordings, ran a publishing house in New York (where he died), and was also able to find time for writing not only the music scores themselves, but books about music in general. He wrote his own autobiography called *Father of the Blues* and various articles. He compiled a list of musicians and their works and generally educated the public about the achievements of Blacks. His fame, however, came mainly from his conducting of the band which he led on tour until he became blind and ceased to perform. He was also an accomplished cornet player. A statue of Handy with his cornet is located in the Handy Park at Memphis, Tennessee.

Handy used African and American characteristics in his music, as reflected in blues features and harmonic outlines. He emphasized the lowered third and seventh, and frequently slurred between the major and minor modes. In addition to the blues, he wrote marches, pieces for the orchestra, piano, voice, chorus and various arrangements for many media.

Among his compositions are: *Memphis Blues, Saint Louis Blues, Beale Street Blues, John Henry Blues, Harlem Blues, The Temple of Music* for chorus, *They That Sow in Tears* for chorus, *Opportunity, Pasadena, When the Black Man Has a Nation of His Own, Who Was the Husband of Aunt Jemima? Mr. Crump, Joe Turner Blues, Careless Love, Hail to the Spirit of Freedom, The Big Stick Blues March, Blue-Destiny Symphony, Afro-American Hymn, Oh, Didn't He Ramble? Black Patti* (of Siseretta

Jones), *East St. Louis, Friendless Blues, Basement Blues, Goin' to See My Sarah, Golden Brown Blues, Hawaiian Guitar* (Blues Album), *Hist de Window, Noah, Nigrita, Mozambique, The Bridegroom Has Done Come, Give Me Jesus, Yellow Dog Blues, Hesitating Blues, John Henry;* the musicals *Opportunity* and *Gettysburg Address;* the collections *Treasury of the Blues, Negro Spirituals* and *Book of Negro Spirituals,* and the book *Negro Music and Musicians.*

FERDINAND (JELLY ROLL) MORTON (1885-1941)

Ferdinand Morton, born Ferdinand La Menthe, was an arranger, composer, conductor, singer and pianist. He was primarily a rag pianist. A native of New Orleans, he died in Los Angeles after having lived in New York and Washington, D.C. While the popularity of rag lasted until about 1915, Morton's life extended beyond this, thereby frustrating his last efforts to prolong the waning span of the rag style while attempting to shift to elements of jazz and blues. Although a talented person who evolved from the classics to jazz, his style was perhaps too classical too soon to be appreciated by the new jazz audiences. For the major changes in concept and style toward classicism *per se* were only accepted after his death.

A member of ASCAP in 1939, Morton was educated in New Orleans through private lessons. He was greatly influenced by Tony Jackson, another rag composer. He practiced the French, African and Spanish dances as well as the technical exercises and feats common to the formal study of music. In addition, Langston Hughes pointed out in his *Famous Negro Music Makers,* that Morton must also have been influenced by the guitar literature which he played from time to time. His band, J. R. Morton's "Red Hot Peppers" and his own composing-performing talents kept him busy in the cabarets, clubs, theatres and recording sessions until his later years. He accompanied and played solos in New York, New Orleans and other cities, after which time he traveled to Washington and California. Much of his venturous styles in music were recorded by the Library of Congress. This recording was labeled *The Saga.*

Among Morton's many works were *The Tiger Rag, The King Porter Stomp, Milnebury Joys, Wolvering Blues, Wild Man Blues, Kansas City Stomp, Mournful Serenade, Shreveport Stomp, Ponchartrain Blues, Jelly Roll Blues, Whinin' Boy Blue, The Pearls, Shoe Shiners' Drag* (London Blues), *The Crave, Buddy Bolden's Blues, Perfect Rag, Frog-i-more Rag, Mama'nita, Grandpa's Spells* and *Original Jelly Roll.*

JAMES P. JOHNSON (1891-1955)

James P. Johnson, pianist-composer of rags and early jazz ballads, was born in New Brunswick, New Jersey. He was hailed as the "Grandfather of Harlem Piano" or "hot piano" and as one who established many of the techniques which distinguished him from the "chaff." Johnson was not only competent in jazz where his reputation was made, but in classical music as well, and he was naturally responsible for influencing the techniques of other musicians. Having been taught by his mother and Bruto

83

Giannini, he in turn taught Thomas Waller, influenced Edward Ellington and generally flourished as an accompanist to Bessie Smith, Ethel Waters, Mamie Smith, Laura Smith and others.

Johnson also made many piano rolls for the player piano. In his style of the "stride" piano, which he originated, he employed techniques of a heavy left hand in alternation of single roots and accented, offbeat chords in an exciting accompaniment to a syncopated melody. He toured Europe with the *Plantation Days* cast, formed his own band at the Clef Club during the 1920's and played at summer resorts, theatres, and night clubs.

Johnson was educated through private study and the New York public schools. In 1926, he became a member of ASCAP. Among his collaborators were Mike Riley, Nelson Cogane and Cecil Mack. His own works included: *Symphonic Harlem, Symphony in Brown, African Drums, Piano Concerto in Ab, Mississippi Moon, Yamacraw* (a Negro *Rhapsody*), *Symphonic Suite on St. Louis Blues, City of Steel, De Organizer* (folk opera), *Kitchen Opera* (operetta), *The Husband* (operetta), *Manhattan Street Scene* (ballet), *Sefronia's Dream* (ballet), *Old Fashioned Love, Don't Cry, Baby, Charleston, If I Could Be With You One Hour Tonight, Stop It, Joe, Mama and Papa Blues, Hey, Hey, Running Wild, Porter's Love Song to A Chambermaid, Snowy Morning Blues, Eccentricity Waltz, Carolina Shout, Keep Off the Grass, Yours All Yours, I was So Weak, Love Was So Strong, Aincha Got Music, Stop That Dog, There Goes My Headache, Rhythm Drums, Caprice Rag, Daintiness Rag, Riff,* and *Sugar Hill.*

CLARENCE WILLIAMS (1898-   )

Clarence Williams, a pianist-composer, arranger, publisher and orchestra leader, was born in New Orleans and traveled to New York at the age of 19. Williams worked in New Orleans in the Main District before joining other jazz groups. Williams did sing, too, but it is reported that his artistry as an accompanist for other singers was greater. He accompanied Ethel Waters, Bessie Smith, Clara Smith, Rev. J. C. Burnette, Peg Leg Howell, Willie Jackson, and George Williams. In addition to performing on stage and in recording sessions, Williams became a pioneer pianist in the small band ensembles and a solo pianist in his own right.

Among his works were *Baby, Won't You Please Come Home, Sugar Blues, I Ain't Gonna Give Nobody None of My Jelly Roll, You Can Have It, I Don't Want It, If You Don't Believe I Love You, Gulf Coast Blues, Squeeze Me, Sister Kate,* and *Royal Garden Blues.*

FLETCHER HENDERSON (1898-1952)

Fletcher Henderson, a native of Cuthbert, Georgia, earned a degree in chemistry from Atlanta University, but also became an accomplished director of orchestras, an accompanist for the Black Swan Troubadours, a song demonstrator and a band director and pianist. A member of the Harlem Symphony, Henderson performed at many of the famous clubs, theaters and cabarets. He accompanied vocal recitals by Bessie Smith,

Clara Smith, Ma Rainey, Ida Cox and Ethel Waters. Henderson's fame, however, came from his innovations in the jazz bands where he led his own ensemble into the "swinging" hot jazz types of New Orleans-style dixieland.

Formal orchestration was his main strength, and according to some sources, he was responsible for setting aside breaks for improvisation within a written composition. He also used the instruments with an individuality uncommon to the mass ensembles before him, wherein sections for instrumental blocks were placed one against the other in alternation. New Yorkers were treated to years of good music through his arrangements and original compositions. He played in the Benny Goodman Orchestra for a few years. In his own band, Fletcher worked with some of the other jazz greats such as Louis Armstrong. Since Henderson produced more arranged works than original works, there was some confusion over which of those attributed to him were really original. Among his own works, however, were *Body and Soul, Down Home Blues* and *King Porter Stomp.*

EDWARD KENNEDY (DUKE) ELLINGTON (1899-   )

Edward Ellington, a composer-pianist, arranger and band leader, was born in Washington, D.C. A fantastic giant of the jazz world, he has bridged the era of Jelly Roll Morton to the world of Ornette Coleman. Having made several tours throughout Europe, the United States and other countries, he has steadily become a legend.

A member of ASCAP since 1953, he was educated in the Washington public schools and studied piano with Henry Grant. Two Black composers whom he favored were Will M. Cook and Will Vodery. Having influenced others, he has continued his efforts through the tradition of jazz, commanding the respect of many and never remaining in one musical position. Wilberforce University, Morgan State College and Milton College are among those who have awarded honorary doctorates to Ellington, and recently, his seventieth birthday celebration was held at the White House.

Ellington's compositional styles ranged from ballad type songs with lyrics to the big-band arrangements for which he is best known. His innovations have even led him into large classical art forms such as the liturgical mass. In addition to his original compositions, he has arranged works by Grieg and Tchaikovsky for jazz orchestras and has also written pieces for voice, piano, band and other media. His collaborators have included the late Toby Hardwick, among others.

Ellington's works include *Bird of Paradise, Black and Tan Fantasy, Don't You Know I Care (Don't You Care to Know), Black, Brown and Beige, Deep South Suite, New World A-Comin', Sepia Panorama, A Drum Is a Woman, Harlem, Suite Thursday, Liberian Suite, Shakespearean Suite, My People, Night Creatures, Non-Violent Integration, Blind Man's Bluff, Sophisticated Lady, Mood Indigo, Creole Love Call, Crescendo in Blue, Christmas Surprise, The Mooche, Prelude to a Kiss, Satin Doll, The Blues, Mass,* Tchaikovsky-Ellington's *Nutcracker Suite,* Grieg-Ellington's *Peer*

Fig. 8. Edward (Duke) Ellington receives another honorary degree from Morgan State College. Courtesy of Maurice Strider.

Gynt Suite; film scores to *Anatomy of a Murder, Jump For Joy, Beggar's Holiday;* and *Paris Blues.*

DANIEL LOUIS (SATCHMO) ARMSTRONG (1900-1971)

Louis Armstrong was a composer-performer of the "hot" jazz tradition. A trumpeter born in New Orleans, Louisiana, he was afforded opportunities at an early age to study various instruments at a Waifs' Home in New Orleans, and to continue his experiences first as an apprentice and later as the top attraction of such famous bands as King Oliver's Creole Band, Fletcher Henderson's Band, Kid Ory's Band and his own groups, the Hot Five and the Sunset Cafe Stompers.

With celebrated artists such as Ma Rainey and Bessie Smith, Dave Brubeck, Duke Ellington and Fats Waller, Armstrong did several recordings, concerts and festival performances. Along with his world tours from Russia to Australia have been his famous concerts in America at the Metropolitan Opera House, Carnegie Hall, the Apollo, and Connie's Inn, to name only a few. Two of the several movies and broadway shows in which Armstrong appeared were *Hello Dolly* with Barbara Streisand, *Pennies From Heaven* with Bing Crosby and *Connie's Hot Chocolates.*

Although more famous for his technical flair and the clear, penetrating sound of his instrument, Armstrong also was instrumental in providing

86

extended compositional skills, ranges and idioms for the trumpet which were uncommon at one time. A leader in a real sense of the oral tradition of Blacks, he often sang to demonstrate this speech communication, and followed it with an imitation on the trumpet. As illustrated in his performances, he made frequent use of ornamentations, improvisation, short trills, some triplets and mainly simplicity of style. However, the spirit of his style influenced perhaps more jazz artists than almost any other pioneer in that field.

Among his arrangements and original works were some 50 recordings including *Everybody Loves My Baby, How Come You Do Me Like You Do, Big Butter and Egg Man From the West; 50 Hot Choruses for Cornet, Weather Bird Rag, Sister Kate, Dippermouth Blues, Potato Head Rag; Some Day; Don't Jive Me; Cornet Chop Suey;* and *Yes I'm in the Barrel.*

THOMAS (FATS) WALLER (1904-1943)

Thomas Waller, a pianist-composer, singer and vaudeville participant, was born in New York and died in Kansas City. An accomplished pianist, he engaged in solo playing, accompanying and recording. He worked as piano accompanist with Florence Mills, Bessie Smith, and also played the organ. Waller was perhaps the first to play jazz publicly on the Hammond and pipe organs. Virtually a legend in the world of jazz, he possessed a good technical facility, and he proved his ability by his frequent performances in both Europe and America. In spite of the short-comings in his personal life and a premature death, he nevertheless left a musical legacy to jazz.

Waller wrote in a mixed style which resembled rag, boogie-woogie and traditional jazz. Some of his music, like that of Joplin and Eubie Blake, was semi-classical and classical. In many of his pieces, the blues penetrated his style, particularly in his vocal music. His mixtures of compositional devices saw *Ring Dem Bells* as being representative of boogies; his vocal pieces were most often ballads, and his *Handful of Keys* was semiclassical. Example 32 outlines some of the features common to Waller's music.

Ex. 32. Waller idioms (introduction, bass and rhythmic excerpts).

Among Waller's works were: *Squeeze Me, My Father, in Your Hands, Honeysuckle Rose, Blue Turning Gray Over You, Zonky, I've Got a Feeling I'm Falling, Keep Shifflin', Ain't Misbehavin', Hot Chocolates, Doin' What I Please, If It Ain't Love, Aincha Glad, Early to Bed* (musical), *Minor Drag, Ring Dem Bells, Viper's Drag, London Suite* and *Handful of Keys.*

WILLIAM COUNT BASIE (1906-   )

William Basie, composer-pianist and conductor, was born in Red Bank, New Jersey. His mother was his first teacher and he also studied with "Fats" Waller. Having served as accompanist in vaudeville productions, he played both piano and organ, and later organized his own orchestra which rivaled contemporary bands, including Ellington's.

Basie once joined with the Bennie Moten Orchestra in Kansas. He also appeared on radio, made records and appeared at numerous hotels, theatres, clubs, jazz festivals and concerts. In 1958, his reputation gained him a place in the Downbeat Hall of Fame.

Also associated with James J. Johnson, "Fats" Waller and pianists of the "stride" piano style of the 1920's and 1930's, his orchestral techniques were more typical of his own interests: uptempos and contrasts from slower march tempos and other techniques borrowed from the era. The "screaming" sensation used by trumpeters (Ala Armstrong) and the equality of writing independent bass and treble melodies were attributed to his pioneer efforts.

Among Basie's works are: *One O'Clock Jump, Every Tub, Good Morning, Blues, John's Idea, Jumping at the Woodside, Basie Boogie, Blues and Sentimental, Gone With the Wind, Two O'Clock Jump, Swingin' the Blues, I Ain't Mad at You, Futile Frustration, Good Bait, Riff Interlude, Miss Thing, Don't You Miss Your Baby?, Panassie Stomp, Shorty George, Out the Window, Hollywood Jump, Nobody Knows, Swingin' at the Daisy Chain* and *I Left My Baby.*

MARY LOU WILLIAMS (1910-   )

Mary Lou Williams, composer-pianist, and arranger, was born in Pittsburgh, Pennsylvania. Called the "Queen of Jazz," she has studied with Ray Lev and has shown further development in England and France while touring and residing there. Now a resident of New York, Williams began a brilliant career around the vaudeville circuits, serving as pianist with the Andy Kirk Band in 1929, and as arranger for the Ellington, Kirk, Crosby, Goodman, Dorsey and Armstrong Bands from the 1930's through 1940's.

As a performer, she possessed a more technically demanding style than many of the pianists before and during her time. Having also performed as solo recitalist, she has given concerts at Town Hall, the New York Philharmonic Hall and at Newport. She spanned early jazz into the newer stages of the 1940's.

Among her compositions are: *Camel Hop, Roll 'Em, Blue Skies* (arrangements), *Zodiac Suite, Cloudy, What's Your Story, Morning Glory?, Ghost of Love, In the Land of Oo Bla Dee, Little Joe from Chicago, Pretty Eyed Baby, Juniper Tree* and *Jazz Opera.*

JOHN (DIZZY) GILLESPIE (1917-   )

John Gillespie, a composer-arranger, trumpeter and "bop" innovator from South Carolina, was instrumental in helping to establish the manner

88

of improvising and planning within the more modern aspects of jazz. Having studied music as a child, Dizzy won a music scholarship to North Carolina, traveled later to Philadelphia and New York, where he began to perform. At first a participant of the swing bands, playing with Earl Hines Band, the Coleman Hawkins Band, and Duke Ellington's Band, he soon formed his own smaller bands.

Gillespie's formal training was more extensive than that of Charlie Parker, who influenced his style. He studied privately, a luxury which Parker could unfortunately not manage because of his neurotic behavior. Nevertheless, under Parker's influence, he was able to abandon some of the traditional methods and formulate a new way of expressing jazz. With his melody extending over longer lines, in contrast to vocally short phrases of blues and ballads, his studied style became more and more instrumental. Yet many of these works incorporated characteristics of the blues. Gillespie was also influenced by collaboration with Ornette Coleman, the younger musician who followed in the modern concept of instrumentation and change.

Dizzy employed independency of instruments within the given orchestration and utilized differences in timbre, intervals and general effects. No one doubted that the shape and position of his damaged trumpet had more than a little to do with these concepts; he yet commanded and gained the respect of his own country and others.

Among his works and arrangements are: *Groovin' High, Jessica's Day, Passport, Leap Frog, Salt Peanuts, My Melancholy Baby, Mohawk, Ow, A Night in Tunisia, Algo Bueno, Dizzy Atmosphere, Anthropology, Behop, Blues and Boogie, Hot House, I Can't Get Started, One Bass Hit, Oo Bop Sha Bam, Two Bass Hits,* and others.

CHARLIE (BIRD) PARKER (1920-1955)

Charlie Parker, composer, arranger and saxophone player, was also an innovator of the difficult and abstract bop style. Jazz, which once placed emphasis upon the melody with short, fragmentary lines, now resorted to long, instrumental tendencies, "breathy" measures and melodic lines several measures long. These, coupled with new harmonic advancements and more freedom of texture, were used to make jazz newer in concept and design.

Although Parker left high school at an early age and joined the band at Clara Monroe's Uptown House and those of Earl Hines and Billy Eckstine, he was at first very musically inept. But he made his way by trial and error, luck and the desire to succeed. With ample help from his fellow musicians, he managed to develop his talents and to grow in spite of his frequent bouts with drugs. Even though Parker acknowledged no formal knowledge of any rules of music, his insight and his talent combined to make his saxophone speak a language of its own. According to Lillian Erlich, he listened to and enjoyed Bartok and Stravinsky, particularly the *Firebird Suite,* and he also spoke fondly of Bach and other classical musicians.

89

Atonal qualities with large intervals placed his compositions into the category of the unusual. The free exchange of popular and art music acted in complementary fashion to one another, and jazz ceased to be just "dance music." Although some of the music retained its characteristic beat for movements typical of the dances, most of these latest developments were also designed for listening and playing.

Among his compositions were: *Now's the Time, Yardbird Suite, Relaxing at Camarillo, Confirmation, Donna Lee, Scrapple From the Apple, Billie's Bounce, Cheryl, Embraceable You, Lover Man, My Little Suede Shoes, Dexterity, Quasimodo, Thriving on a Riff, Anleu-cha, Count-Down, Little Willie Leaps, This Love of Mine, Just Friends, Cherokee, Ornithology* and others.

THELONIUS MONK (1920?-   )

Thelonius Monk, a pianist-composer born in Rocky Mount, North Carolina, and who now lives in New York, is a jazz innovator directly associated with Dizzy Gillespie and Charlie Parker. Monk was also influenced by the styles of Earl Hines, James P. Johnson, Teddy Wilson, Fats Waller, and Willie (the Lion) Smith. A fusion of the new with the older styles, his compositional devices were characterized by the "blurps and bleeps" of the keyboard's outer extremities of sound and touch, block chords and dissonances, and a feeling of atonalism, abstractness and novelty.

Monk grew to this stage somewhat gradually, as his style was originally traditional. His own experimentations began approximately the same time as Parker's. By the 1950's, his style was molded into newer concepts and were demonstrated at the Apollo, at festivals and on recordings.

At first not accepted, his jazz results were really no more irregular than those of Charles Ives in art music. There were those who felt that jazz, like its followers, should not be restricted and should not be allowed to voice the harmony of dissent in other than a traditional sound. Yet the new music continued to be influenced by its environment as well as ideas from art music. The more sophisticated intellectualism of musical features also encouraged the jazz players to conform to their own individual capacities.

Called the most important figure after Ellington's era, Monk has been featured in *Time* magazine, *Current Biography,* and *Downbeat.* Of his music, there is yet a feeling for the blues, having been versed in the "hotness" of jazz. There is the difficulty of bop, and the harmonies of the progressive era merge to provide an ultimate outcome. His compositions denote improvisation, freedom of time, with the appearance of form, variation and other simple or multi-sectional forms.

Among his works are: *Round About Midnight, Crisscross, Misterioso, Off Minor, Evidence, Ruby, In Walked Bud, Blue Monk, I Mean You, Hackensack, Epistrophy, My Dear, Fifty-second Street Theme,* and *Well You Needn't.*

Fig. 9. William (Billy) Taylor.

WILLIAM (BILLY) TAYLOR (1921-   )

William Taylor, a composer, author, conductor, pianist, educator and business executive, was born in Greenville, North Carolina. He later moved to Washington, D.C. and eventually to New York City. Educated at Virginia State College as a student of Undine Moore, he later served as pianist with the Ben Webster Quartet and the Cozy Cole Quintet (in *Seven Lively Hits,* broadway musical). He toured with Redman in Europe and has otherwise remained in demand for concerts at major institutions and halls throughout Europe and the Americas. A recipient of honorary degrees from Fairfield University and Virginia State College, he has been hailed as one of the greatest jazz composer-performers also because of the fine work which he has exhibited with his own trios, duos and other ensembles.

91

Taylor has performed as the music director of the David Frost Television Show. He has taught at the Manhattan School of Music and other institutions, and has lectured about jazz in a jazzmobile. He was perhaps the first to be sponsored on an NBC broadcast called *The Subject of Jazz.* He has arranged scores for several personalities, including Ethel Smith and Dizzy Gillespie, and has served as vice-president of the Musicians Clinic in New York City. In addition, Taylor has been an appointee to the New York State Commission on the Cultural Resources and an advisor on jazz at the Lincoln Center, among other commendations.

Having begun with the "bop" tradition, Taylor contributes to jazz in emotion, style and competence and experiments with other styles and techniques common to the twentieth century. Mostly of the tonal variety, his compositions emphasize melody, independency of melody against clearly defined harmony and ornamental improvisation of the highest caliber. Featuring intricately difficult cross-rhythms and technically unique lines in contrary motion, he also employs chord clusters sparingly, occasional dissonances and contrapuntal implications. His style, however, is ever-developing.

A knowledgeable and scholarly musician, Taylor has written 12 books on jazz, some 300 songs and manuals of instruction. He has composed: *Basic Bebop Instruction, Dixieland Piano Solos, Mambo Piano Solos, Ragtime Piano Solos, Midnight Piano, Cuban Cutie, Ever So Easy, Dido, Just the Thought of You, You Tempt Me, It's a Grand Night for Swinging, A Bientot, Capricious, Rosetta* (arr.), *Sweet Lorraine* (arr.), *Dog Zigity Rag, Biddy's Beat, Tune For Tex, Feeling Frisky, Theodora,* and others.

WILLIE (BILL) HARRIS (1925-   )

Willie Harris, born in Nashville, North Carolina, and currently residing in Washington, D.C., is one of the few composer-performers for guitar in the field of jazz. A teacher at Federal City College, he began the study of the guitar after venturing into trumpet techniques and a variety of other professions before concentrating on music. Educated by his mother on the piano, as well as by members of the Washington Junior College and Sophocles Papas, he has studied both classical and popular guitar and has generally made a name for himself on the east coast. Harris has composed and performed for numerous concerts, festivals, institutions, and clubs and has made recordings.

Although primarily of the established key concept, his efforts show traditional techniques interspersed with contemporary harmonies. However, the bulk of his music is centered around the "bop" era and the modern styles of "funk." His techniques include chromatics, up-tempos, a slight obscurity of keys (not atonalism), parallelisms and improvisational features (written and unwritten). His varieties of natural guitar sounds are both fascinating and pleasing. An excerpt from his *Ethyl* is shown in Example 33.

Ex. 33. *Ethyl*, Harris. Used by permission of composer.

Among Harris' original and arranged works are: *Ethyl, Blue Angel, K. C. Shuffle, Possessed, Dreaming, Ivanhoe, Your Majesty, The Harris Touch, Jazz Chords, Jazz Introductions, Jazz Endings, Octave Study, Runs and Chords, Intaglio, Elizabeth's Card, Baker's Dozen, Peg O' My Heart, Blue Moon, Satin Doll, Flying Home, Don't Blame Me;* and others.

JOSEPH J. KENNEDY, JR. (1923-   )

Joseph Kennedy, Jr., composer, violinist, composer and arranger was born in Pittsburgh, Pennsylvania, but moved later to Richmond, Virginia. Educated at Carnegie Mellon University, Virginia State College and Duquesne University (where he received the Master's Degree), his first teachers were family members. He has since been influenced by the late Jimmie Lunceford. His association with Ahmad Jamal in composing, arranging, conducting and performing on recordings and at other concerts has added to his practical experiences. He has performed at Carnegie Music Hall, the Arts Festival in Birmingham, Michigan, and the Jazz Festivals at Hampton Institute.

As an active art musician, Kennedy performs with the Richmond Symphony Orchestra and conducts various ensembles, having served as guest conductor at the Mid-West National Band and Orchestra Clinic in 1968. Also in 1965, he conducted the Cleveland Summer Symphony in a premiere of his own work, the *Suite for Trio and Orchestra.* As an educator, he teaches at John Marshall High and Virginia Commonwealth.

Although Kennedy has composed traditional jazz compositions and art music, he has done other works during the contemporary period which border on third stream music. This is particularly true of his *Dialogue for Flute, Cello and Piano,* which he composed for Trio Pro Viva. His reputation, however, has been established as a jazz composer of a modern style similar to the "bop" tradition, merging with techniques from the early progressives. His harmony is related to that of Bud Powell who moderately restricts the music to contemporary practices within a tonal frame. Steeped in the emotion of the blues and other forms, Kennedy also employs ornamentations and frequent altered sevenths, dissonances and free-flowing rhythms. His clear comprehensible forms vary from ballad styles and three-part forms to that of the free fantasy. Two excerpts of his writing are shown in Example 34.

Fig. 10. Joseph Kennedy.

Ex. 34. *Serious Moods* and *Somewhat Eccentric* (first measures), Kennedy. Used by permission of Hema Music Corporation.

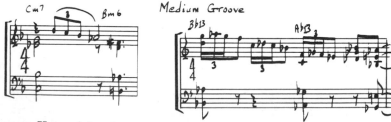

Among Kennedy's other works are: *A Lazy Atmosphere, Tempo for Two, Surrealism, You Can Be Sure, The Fantastic Vehicle, Illusions Opticas, Nothing to Fret About, Disenchantment, Hynoptic, Serious Moods, Charming Attitudes, Somewhat Eccentric, Suite for Trio and Orchestra, Dialogue for Flute, Cello and Piano,* and others.

The composers of jazz were responsible for maintaining many aspects of Africanism in American music and for influencing all musical forms while developing a newer art form. They also paved the way for the later developments and elevations in contemporary jazz itself. These musicians exhausted the stylistic elements of the Baroque and Romantic periods in their diligent penetration of all music, and have made significant gains in the Modern Period.

X
ART MUSIC:
ITS DEFINITION, TRENDS, AND COMPOSERS

Simultaneous with developments in American jazz, Blacks produced brilliantly in the area of art music. Originally designed for the society's elite, art music, or classical music, created a hierarchy and a stratification between high and low economic classes of society. Because the majority of the American Blacks were of the lowest economic strata, art music traditionally excluded them. Yet their talents and efforts directed many to be successful in this classical art form.

Definition

Based on an imitation of the "classicism" found in early Greece and Rome, art music became intellectual, academic, traditional, or that which had "withstood the test of time". It stressed the abstract and readily aesthetic response to an appreciation of higher values. Also used to denote the musical period of the late eighteenth century, the word "classical" evolved around the time of Franz Joseph Haydn (1732-1809), Wolfgang Mozart (1756-1791), early Ludwig van Beethoven (1770-1827) and George Bridgetower, a Black contemporary.

Art music was a highly involved system which demanded of its listeners as much concentration and knowledge of its historical and theoretical aspects as it did from its composers and performers. Unlike African communal participation, the response of listeners was passive rather than active, while the performer was spotlighted in the role of reenacting or recreating the work of a composer. It also concentrated upon the realization of history through "correct" or exactly prescribed performance within the given styles or periods. Unlike popular music whose beginning was less formal in its restricted habits of performance and composition, the history of art music was once collected and formed most directly by the Catholic Church. Therefore, most of western music history depended upon a church which attempted to codify a large body of compositions by purging the trite and the secular from the religious (popular versus art music).

Later art music further set itself apart from the popular forms by use of certain rigidities in maintaining specific timbres for some of its forms. The orchestra was divided into strings, woodwinds, brasses and percussions, with strings predominating. Symphonies made use of these orchestrations as opposed to the chamber quality of winds and percussion common to popular orchestras. Voices were likewise divided into soprano, alto, tenor and bass; subdivisions within these voices were coloratura, lyric or mezzo soprano, contralto, contratenor and baritone. Even though instruments assumed characteristic styles common to their own technical capacities in a given era, all instruments before the modern period imitated the "singing" style of the voice. Composers were aware of the ranges and characteristics of style common to instruments and voices, and wrote accordingly.

Even though the history of this music was based on many African contributions and the universality of music in general, this fact was generally omitted in the documents important to the study of art music in modern Europe and America. Consequently, art music in America became unrightfully associated with the educated, the privileged and the White European. Unnecessarily placed on a pedestal above the minds and reaches of most Blacks, it assumed a separation of races. This created a separation of certain music from a certain class of people, and was yet another reason why Blacks have been omitted from the modern history of music. It also explained why such a piece as Debussy's *Cakewalk* was catalogued within art music while Scott Joplin's *Maple Leaf* was placed in jazz.

Forms

Black composers in America used forms already established in art music. The structures of art music were, in part, based on popular European music derived from dances, vocal and instrumental forms. Some absolute (abstract) or descriptive forms were conceived from original or traditional pieces such as motets, cannons, gigues, bourrees, gavottes, preludes, intermezzos, etudes and symphonic poems. Some of the most common forms which contained several movements were: the sonata, a piece written for one to three instruments; opera, a music-drama for vocalists, dancers and orchestra; ballet, a piece for dancers and orchestra; the mass, a liturgical piece in celebration of the Last Supper; and the fugue, an imitative piece based upon a theme which is highly developed, and greatly resembling the antiphonal quality of a call and response.

Neo-Romantic Composers of the Modern Period

The modern period of art music consisted of various styles built upon formulas of past eras as well as the more dissonant techniques of the modern century. It also reflected a continuation of German romanticism. Without question, the latter period served as the model for the majority of the earliest composers discussed in this chapter, with its emphasis upon praise of beauty and nature, love of humanistic approaches and especially nationalism.

HENRY (HARRY) T. BURLEIGH (1866-1949)

Harry T. Burleigh, a baritone-composer, arranger, and teacher was born Henry T. Burleigh in Erie, Pennsylvania, and lived to the age of eighty-three before he died in Stamford, Connecticut. His life began at Reconstruction and lasted well into the second stage of Black musical developments. His own style reflected both of these ages in that he forged ahead in the popular minstrel shows while maintaining representative works in the field of art music within the modern period.

He studied with Max Spicker, John White, Rubin Holdmark, Christian Fritsch and others. While at the Conservatory, Burleigh also came under the influence of Anton Dvorak, the Czech composer who inspired America to use indigenous material such as the Black and Indian folk songs, rather than to continue within the inspirations and forms of the European tradition.

A capable baritone as well as a good composer, Burleigh found the time to sing spirituals and other songs for Dvorak, who in turn, promoted the use of spirituals by including thematic or similar emotional material in his *New World Symphony*. Another for whom Burleigh sang was Darius Milhaud, the French composer who came to America during the early 1900's and diligently attended jazz clubs and other places where Black music was performed. Milhaud showed this influence in some of his works such as *La Creation du Monde*.

In addition to his work at the Conservatory, Burleigh gained a reputation for his fine musicianship at the Temple Emmanuel (Jewish) and the Saint George's Church in New York (where he became a soloist, much to the chagrin of the White congregation). Of his voice, some reviews of the day noted:

Honor to Negro Spirituals and to Harry T. Burleigh. His voice, robust and clear, rang out in joyous strains of the hymn . . . front rank of the musicians of our time — *International Negro Press*, June 1936.

Having won many awards for both his composition and his singing, among which was the Spingarn Medal given by the National Association of Colored People, he also earned other prizes and gave concert tours. He was the musical spokesman for Black achievements.

Burleigh wrote innumerable songs, arranged many spirituals and popular songs, and edited a few volumes of spirituals and ballads. One book so edited contained twenty-one songs by H. C. Work, Stephen Foster and others. They were also representative of his own style of writing. Burleigh's style consisted of tonal Romantic types of simple harmonies and techniques. Among his works were: *Young Warrior; The soldier, Oh Brothers Lift Your Voices; Love's Garden; Five Songs* (text Lawrence Hope); *Ethiopia Saluting the Colors; The Grey Wolf; Saracen Songs; One Year; Little Mother of Mine; Carry Me Back to the Pine Wood; A Corn Song; Just Because; If Life Be a Dream; I Love My Jean; From the Southland; The Glory of the Day was in Her Face; Keep a Good Grip on de Hoe; Mammy's Lil Baby; Her Eyes; Twin Pools; Balm in Gilead; Ain't Going to Study War No Mo'; Behold that Star; By an' By; Couldn't Hear Nobody Pray; De Blin' Man Stood on de Road an' Cried; De Gospel Train; Deep River; You May Bury Me in de Eas'*; and *A Jubilee*.

97

HARRY LAWRENCE FREEMAN (1869-1954)

Harry L. Freeman, a little known and little publicized composer, was born in Cleveland, Ohio, and was buried in New York after a career of art music and popular involvement. Primarily interested in drama and music together, he was credited with the organization of the Freeman School of Music in 1911, the Freeman School of Grand Opera in 1923, and with the founder of the Negro Opera Company in 1920. Because it was uncommon for Black opera singers to join unions or any organizations for Whites, and because of the stereotype that Blacks "could sing music but not necessarily opera," his work was highly significant.

A winner of the Harmon Award in 1930, and conductor of many concerts and the pageant at Chicago during the World's Fair in 1934, Freeman was cited as being the first Black composer in the United States to conduct a symphony orchestra in a rendition of his own work (*O Sing a New Song*) which he directed at Minnesota in 1907. He was also cited as being the first Black to write fourteen grand style operas. Freeman studied theory with J. H. Beck, piano with E. Shonert and Carlos Sobrino. From 1902 to 1904 he taught at Wilberforce, and from 1910 to 1913 at the Salem School in North Carolina.

Among his works were: *O Sing a New Song* (orchestra); *The Martyr; Valdo; African Krall; Octaroon; The Tryst; The Prophecy; Athalia; The Plantation; Vendetta; American Romance* (jazz opera); *Voodoo; Leah Kleschma; Uzziah; Zuzuland* (tetralogy: first part, 2150 pages); *The Slave* (ballet for orchestral and choral ensemble); *If Thou Didst Love; Whither;* and others.

CLARENCE CAMERON WHITE (1880-1960)

Clarence Cameron White, violinist, composer and educator, was born in Clarksville, Tennessee. Educated at Oberlin College, White studied violin with Zacharwitsch, won two Rosenwald Fellowships and was awarded honorary degrees from Atlanta University and Wilberforce. He also was awarded the David Bispham Award for his opera *Quanga* and a Harmon Foundation Medal. After having served as a teacher in public schools and music studios in Boston, he served as chairman of the music department at West Virginia State College in 1924, as director of music at the Hampton Institute, and taught at the Washington Conservatory.

As guest artist with Samuel Coleridge-Taylor, the Black European composer, White toured the United States and London for three years. He concertized extensively, organized programs for the National Recreational Association and wrote articles (one of which was a study of Bridgetower, another Black European). He was a member of ASCAP, which he joined in 1924. His genuine interest in his profession coupled with his intense desire to devote more time to performance and the writing of music, forced him to resign from the chairmanship of Hampton Institute after only three years. Eventually, he settled in New York where he died.

A talented composer of the neo-Romantic style, he also employed the

98

use of modern techniques. White wrote various compositions for vocal and instrumental media and during his lifetime, he was hailed as "America's foremost composer of opera."

Among his works were: *Two Pieces; Opus 60 for Piano; Bandanna Sketches* (Slave songs); *Five Songs; Improvisation; Levee Dance; Camp Song; Fleurette; Quanga* (music drama in 3 acts); *Plantation Song; Dance Caprice; The Question; Tuxedo; Nobody Knows de Trouble I've Seen* (and numerous other spiritual arrangements); *Piece for Strings and Timpani; A Night in Sans Souci* (ballet); *Violin Concerto No. 2 in E minor; Symphony in D minor;* and *From the Cotton Fields.*

FLORENCE PRICE (1888-1953)

Florence Price, composer, pianist, organist and educator, was born at Little Rock, Arkansas, and died in Chicago, Illinois. She was educated at the New England Conservatory, by Cutter, Chadwick, and Converse; at the American Conservatory; at Chicago Musical College; at Chicago Teachers College; at Central YWCA College; at the Lewis Institute; and at Chicago University. Price also was influenced by her teachers Henry Dunkan, Charles Denner, A. Anderson and others. Her teaching career was spent at Shorter College, Clark University. Her memberships included the NAACC and the ASCAP organizations, and among her awards was the coveted Wanamaker Prize.

Florence Price wrote many compositions and arrangements for various media. Her works were performed by herself, Margaret Bond and others. Her style was Romantic, and consisted of some technically difficult devices as well as smaller designs intended for intermediate levels.

Among her works were the following: *Symphony in E minor* (Wannamaker Prize); *Symphonic Tone Poem; Piano Concerto; Violin Concerto; Quintet for Piano and Strings; Concert Overture* (based on Black spirituals); *The Wind and the Sea; Three Little Negro Dances; Lincoln Walks at Midnight; Rhapsody for Piano and Orchestra; Negro Folksongs in Counterpoint, a String Quarter; Moods for Flute, Clarinet, and Piano; Organ Sonata; Passacaglia and Fugue for Organ; My Soul's Been Anchored in de Lord,* and many other arrangements of spirituals.

HALL JOHNSON (1888-1970)

Hall Johnson, a composer, author, conductor, and arranger, was a resident of New York City at the time of his unfortunate death in his apartment on April 30, 1970. Born in Athens, Georgia, he was the recipient of many awards and other honors. On Sunday, April 19, a Musical Tribute to Hall Johnson was given at which many local and national musicians and other dignitaries performed in his honor. At the occasion, Major John Lindsay presented Dr. Johnson with New York City's "highest and most coveted award," The Handel Award; the John Motley Chorus sang his cantata of *Music in Negro Idiom,* the *Son of Man;* and the Carl Fisher Music Company was among others who presented him with honors.

During his lifetime, Johnson received an honorary Mus. D. degree from the Philadelphia Music Academy as well as countless other awards. Having studied with Percy Goetschius and others, his education was received at Allen University, Atlanta University, Knox Institute, the University of Pennsylvania and the New York Institute of Musical Art. Johnson also specialized in languages such as French and German, but his primary emphasis was music. A member of ASCAP, his specialties became the violin, voice and composition.

He concertized on radio, television and films and also recorded many songs. He played the violin with the Vernon Castle Orchestra, served as arranger and musical director for the Broadway production *Green Pastures,* and as writer of the music for the Broadway stage score *Run Little Chilin.* In his many tours, he performed with the Festival for Negro Choruses of Los Angeles which he organized in 1936. He formed the Hall Johnson Choir in 1925, and toured the United States and Europe for the State Department in 1951.

Like those before and after him, Johnson developed a greatness from within which spoke of the heritage of the Black spirituals. Having been influenced by those older Blacks who constantly sang the songs around him, he developed an early sensitivity for the musical heritage and gained a reputation for his writing as well as the performance of his songs.

His style, mainly Romantic and homophonic, ranged from the somber and the religious to the forthright gay styles and pleasantries of life. His spirituals showed a command of the keyboard and vocal line, as well as of ornamentation. Generally, his lines of such songs also used unadorned vocal lines and simplicity of form, although technical and emotional aspects ranged high. His other works also reflected his command of instrumental characteristics and their inherent possibilities. His most exciting developments, however, stemmed from the enthusiasm which he used in his efforts to develop and promote the Black spirituals.

Among his works were: *Book of Negro Spirituals; Honor, Honor; Oh What a Beautiful City; Steal Away; His Name So Sweet; The Green Pastures* (a collection of 25 spirituals from the play); *Take My Mother Home* (based on a narrative from St. John); *I Cannot Stay Here By Myself* (a slave's lament); *Tradition* (arr.); *Run Little Chilun* (stage score); *Son of Man* (cantata); *Fi-Yer* (Fire), and many others for various media.

ROBERT NATHANIEL DETT (1882-1943)

Robert Nathaniel Dett, pianist, composer, arranger, and educator, was born in Drummondsville, Canada, and died at Battle Creek, Michigan. Dett was educated at the Oliver Willis Halstead Conservatory in Lockport, New York; at Oberlin College (where he received the B.M. and Mus.D. degrees); at Columbia University, the University of Pennsylvania, Harvard University, the Eastman School of Music (where he received the M.M. degree) and at the Niagara Falls Collegiate Institute. Two honorary Doctorates were given to him by Howard University and Oberlin Conservatory.

100

s: 50c to $2.50.   One-half space reserved for white people.

Sale Beginning   Tickets on Sale Beginning Jan.
26th, for white   26th, for colored people Yates
people at Cable Piano Co. **-- The --** & Milton Drug Store, Auburn
                    Ave. and Butler St. Y. M. C. A.

HAMPTON INSTITUTE
GLEE CLUB

—With—
R. NATHANIEL DETT
Famous Composer-Pianist
—Directing—

Fig. 11. Robert Nathaniel Dett. Courtesy of Hampton Institute Library.

Highly trained, Dett joined ASCAP in 1925 and continued to create a legend for himself in his own time.

His many professional positions included church pianist in Niagara Falls between 1898 and 1903; director of music at Lane College between 1908 and 1911, at Lincoln Institute from 1911 to 1913, at Bennett College in 1937 and finally at Hampton Institute in Virginia where he was a teacher of Dorothy Maynor, soprano. He was credited with founding the American Art Society. He served as a conductor of many choral ensembles and wrote articles and edited many collections. In addition, Dr. Dett was the deserving recipient of various awards, among which were the Harmon Foundation Award, Francis Boott Music Prize at Harvard, Bowdoin Literary Prize, and the Palm and Ribbon Royal Belgian Band Award.

Although some people still did not consider his music worthwhile, Dett was nevertheless a composer of reputable qualifications and talent whose works generated his success. From contemporary newspaper articles at that time, captions revealed Dett's professionalism and respect, and cast light upon the subject of his competence and acceptance into the world of art music. In part, the news media has stated:

Dr. R. Nathaniel Dett in Rochester Attracts Attention   *Afro-American,* 1934

We are a great people with strange dreams and a wonderful heritage lost somewhere in the years between. . . . (Dett)   *Afro-Dispatch,* 1934

Oratorio by Dett Played by Symphony (*The Ordering of Moses*).
Kansas City Call, 1937

As a matter of one-man's opinion . . . . one of the most thrilling . . . (said of Dett's Choir performance by Douglass Gordon)

Dett was a totally competent and praiseworthy composer of his day. His general style of writing was quite organized and refined, as well as both established and experimental. For his works he received honors for producing the first large oratorio to be based on motifs of Black folk music. This production was a Cincinnati Broadcast with Eugene Goosens conducting 350 voices. He was also chosen by the Rochester Exposition to furnish music for a drama then in progress (Pathways of Progress) which he prepared in three weeks and which was termed a "spendid effect." His final virtues of choral conducting and management were beyond reproach. Vivian McBrier, for her doctoral dissertation at Catholic University, has further reviewed the works and worth of the man in an extensive study.

Although Dett composed for several media, he did equally well in both vocal and instrumental styles. In addition, he composed and arranged compositions for vocal combinations, and for media such as piano and other instruments. Dett's style was virtually Romantic, but rhythmically and harmonically exciting in his frequent and refreshing use of technically demanding material. His controlled balance of voices and complete knowledge of instrumentation attested to his virtuosity. Chromaticisms or other techniques were used in various ternary, operatic or symphonic forms of art music. Some of his music also bordered on popular varieties, particularly such as the familiar *Juba Dance* with its ragtime-like bass and danc-ing, dotted melodies. Yet the calmness and technical style of the second section resembled the traditional song form styles of the 1900's. An ex-cerpt of the latter work is shown in Example 35:

Ex. 35. *Juba Dance,* Dett. Copyright 1913 by Summy-Birchard Company, Evans-ton, Illinois. Copyright renewed. All Rights Reserved. Used by permission.

Among Dett's other works were: *Noon Siesta; To a Closed Casement; A Bayou Garden; Legend of the Atoll; American the Beautiful* (1918); *Drink to me Only with Thine Eyes;* the *Daybreak Charioteer; Parade of the Jasmine Bannera; Oh Hear the Lambs A-Cryin'; Ponpons and Fens; Now Rest Beneath Night's Shadows; The Ordering of Moses* (Biblical folk scene of soli, chorus, and orchestra); *Go Not from Me, O God; Sit Down, Servant, Sit Down; O Lord, the Hardwon Miles; Magnolia* (piano suite) *Enchantment* (piano suite); *In the Bottoms* (piano suite) *Don't be Weary Traveler* (motet, Francis Boot Prize); *The Chariot Jubilee* (for tenor solo, chorus and orchestra); *An American Sampler* (orchestra); *Ramah* (violin); *I'm so Glad Trouble don't Last Always; Sinners Won't you Hear; Deep River; I'll Never Turn Back No More; Listen to the Lambs* (women's voices); *Who Made Thee?; Walk Ye in God's Love; Religious Folk Songs of the Negro* (edited); *Dett Collection of Spirituals* (4 volumes); and other works.

CAMILLE NICKERSON

Camille Nickerson, noted pianist-singer and educator, was born in New Orleans, Louisiana. She now resides in Washington, D.C. Having be-gun an early study of music with her father, William Nickerson, she at-tended the Oberlin Conservatory where she received the Bachelor of Music and Master of Music degrees. She later did post-graduate work at the Juilliard School of Music and at Teachers College, Columbia University.

As an educator, Camille Nickerson began teaching at the William Nickerson School of Music in New Orleans. In 1926, however, she moved

Fig. 12. Camille Nickerson.

Fig. 13. William Dawson.

to Howard University School of Music in Washington, D.C., where she was eventually elevated to the rank of professor. By 1930, her talents as a composer and research scholar won her many honors and awards, among which was a Rosenwald Fellowship for Study in the field of Creole Folk Music of Louisiana. Through her diligence in this area, an impressive legacy of early folk music from Latin influences was documented in her writings, depicting themes of romance; she also wrote compositional arrangements of Creole songs for choral ensembles and solo voice, many of the latter of which she herself performed in innumerable concerts at halls, institutions and festivals throughout the United States and Europe.

Her compositions show tonal examples of both homophonic and slight polyphonic trends. Highly sensitive in lyrical and harmonic concepts, the beauty of the music is highlighted within simplicity and delicacy of form and style, yet very concretely woven to support the unusual Creole poetry, rhythms of the habernera, or simple lines of melodic emphasis.

Among her compositions are: *Mazelle Zizi; Christmas Everywhere; The Women of the USA; Five Creole Songs* (*Chere Moi, Lemme Toi; Lizette, To Quitte la Plaine; Danse Conni Conne; Fais Dodo* and *Micheu Banjo*); *When Love Is Done; Aurore Pradere; Suzanne, Belle Femme;* and *Spring Song.*

WILLIAM LEVI DAWSON (1899   )

William Levi Dawson, a composer, conductor, trombonist and educator, was born in Anniston, Alabama, near Tuskegee Institute, Alabama, where he now resides. Once the organizer and chairman of the Department of Music at the famed Tuskegee Institute, Dawson ran away from home at an early age in order to attend the School. Thereafter, he made his way to the Horner Institute of Fine Arts in Missouri, the American Conservatory of Music in Chicago (where he received the Master's degree), and eventually became the first trombonist of the Chicago Civic Symphony Orchestra where he remained for several seasons.

Dawson has served as director of innumerable choirs and orchestral ensembles while lecturing and traveling extensively in the United States and abroad. He has been so effective a conductor of the Tuskegee Choir that he was invited to perform at Radio City, Carnegie Hall and the White House. In addition, his conducting ability has placed him in demand as guest conductor at many festivals, contests and institutions. He conducted the Fisk University Choir in a performance of Coleridge-Taylor's *Hiawatha,* the Fredonia New York State Choir and Orchestra in a performance of his *Symphony,* and the Talladega Choir in Dett's *Ordering of Moses.*

One wonders why Dawson withdrew from the extended forms of art music and later concentrated solely on the vocal medium of folk spirituals. He had composed for small chamber ensembles, piano, trombone and other media. His bulk of compositions, however, showed many arrangements in the vocal idiom. Within the folk idiom were seen both contrapuntal and homophonic techniques.

105

As a winner of the Wanamaker Contest Prize in 1930, for his song and orchestral compositions, and a winner of the Chicago Daily News prize for the Contest of Band Directors in 1929, Dawson still suffered setbacks in his profession. For example, at the time of high praise during the popularity of his *Symphony,* he was called upon to defend his style of writing, to which he responded that he had not tried to imitate any other composer, but attempted to "be just myself, a Negro. To me, the finest compliment that could be paid my *Symphony* when it had its premiere is that it unmistakably is not the work of a white man. I want the audience to say: only a Negro could have written that." No one asked Milhaud and Ravel or anyone else to defend their music, as it was expected of them to compose art music in any style they chose. However, Dawson's composition was so beautifully constructed and well presented that his critics could not contain themselves.

Another adverse circumstance to his case was the fact that Dawson was instructed to sit in the balcony of the Horner Institute auditorium while his own pieces were being performed upon the date of his graduation from the School. Even though the pieces won first prize, he was nevertheless not allowed to walk on the stage in order to receive the applause or acknowledgement. Despite this, however, William Dawson's ability, hard work and excellence of achievement brought eventual respect and acceptance of his talent finally realized by the awards and subsequent honors bestowed upon him. There was no question but that William Dawson knew his work as both conductor and composer, for he performed accordingly each time he came before the public.

One of the highlights of his career was undoubtedly the completion and performance of his *Negro Folk Symphony,* which was presented in Philadelphia with Leopold Stokowsky as conductor. *The Folk Symphony* was written during the early 1930's and consisted of three movements. Also of the Romantic style, its homophonic texture was off-set by other features of call and response, overlapping, and motivic themes. His keen sense of balance in both the vocal and orchestral works were exciting and well written. In the *Symphony,* the organization was built around the Black spirituals as seen below:

FIRST MOVEMENT:	(Introduction) *The Bond of Africa,* based on spiritual *Oh My Little Soul is Gwine Shine*
SECOND MOVEMENT:	*Hope in the Night,* reflecting a slave's lament; sorrow and despair; children's dance, scherzo; abandonment of care.
THIRD MOVEMENT:	*O le' Me Shine* *Hallelujah, Been Down to the Sea* *O le' Me Shine*

Dawson's style of writing encompassed many technical devices common to art music as well as to Black folk songs. Generally of the Romantic style, using tonal centers, various overlapping and syncopated and irregularly accented rhythms were typical of his music. His *I Wan' to Be Ready*

106

for mixed voices was published in 1967, a composition consisting of four to seven voice parts. With the additional use of pedal points and other suspended tones, Dawson used polytonalities which added to the pleasure of the work. The beginning measures are seen in Example 36.

Ex. 36. *I Wan' to Be Ready*, Dawson. Copyright 1967 by William L. Dawson. Tuskegee Institute, Alabama. International Copyright Secured. Printed in the U.S.A. All rights reserved. Neil Kjos Music Co., Park Ridge, Ill., sole Distributor.

Among Dawson's best works are: *Ansioso* (*Anxiety*) *For Piano; Scherzo* (for orchestra); *Jump Back, Honey, Jump Back; The Mongrel Yank; Negro Folk Symphony No. 1; Out in the Fields; Untitled Composition* (Moorland Room, Howard University); *Trio for Piano; Soon Ah Will Be Done Wid de Trouble of de World,* mixed male voices; *Good News,* mixed male voices; *Oh What a Beautiful City,* mixed voices; *There is a Balm in Gilead,* mixed male, female voices; *Deep River; Steal Away,* mixed male; *Hail Mary;* mixed male voices; *Swing Low, Sweet Chariot,* mixed male, female voices; *Mary Had a Baby; Ezekiel Saw de Wheel; Zion's Walls; Behold the Star; Lover's Plighted; A Negro Work Song* for orchestra; and other songs, both arranged and original.

JOHN WESLEY WORK III (1901-1967)

John Wesley Work III, a composer, theorist, vocalist, educator and humanitarian, was born in Tullahoma, Tennessee. A true scholar and friend of all people, Work inspired those who met him to imitate his intense love of life, of worthwhile endeavors and of music. A proud, honest and conscientious teacher of legendary significance, he instilled a willingness to work and a need to achieve.

Educated at the Fisk School (when Fisk was a high school) and at Fisk University, he also studied at the Institute of Musical Art, at Columbia University (where he received the Master's degree) and at Yale University. His professional career was spent in compiling music history through the study of spirituals and in writing scores as well as articles about music.

Work remained at Fisk from 1926-1966, variously serving as theorist-composer, and as director of the famed Jubilee Singers and the

Fisk Men's Glee Club. In addition, he served for five years as chairman of the Fisk University Department of Music. Upon his retirement from Fisk in 1966, he could count 39 years of dedicated service. On one occasion, Work was awarded an honorary doctorate by Fisk University, who loved him as he loved the University. His tireless energies brought many rewards and honors for the University and his diligency in striving for perfection of his ideas and thoughts on Black music or music in general was of flawless quality.

His writing began when he was in high school at which time he composed *Mandy Lou*. He received a prize from the Fellowship of American Composers in 1946 for still another work, *The Singers*. Considered by some to be his most significant composition, it was based on a poem by Henry Wadsworth Longfellow and was originally scored for chorus, baritone and orchestra.

After a trip to Haiti in 1945, Work returned home to write a piece based upon the music of that country, *Yenvalou*, which was once performed in 1959 by the total Symphony at Saratoga, N.Y. Work subsequently wrote another version which was scored for two pianos and was performed at Fisk in 1947. Another of his works, *Golgotha*, was also presented by the Fisk University Choir during the 1949 Festival, a work based on a poem by Arna Bontemps.

John Work's forte was his choral and vocal solo works, and he excelled in both conducting and writing. Yet his other works contained music of worth, and as compiled and discussed by Simona Atkins and Dorris Williams, totalled well over 100 compositions. His works were written for piano, chamber ensembles, chorus and other media, but the bulk was choral in nature.

While his basic writing appeared in the Romantic vein, some of the elements used were contrapuntal, closely interwoven chords of altered varieties, and jazz. While the instrumental pieces showed a characteristic instrumental idiom they were more often based on a vocal linear concept, or singable lines.

Some works incorporated a gospel-like spirit of a recitative while others moved in syncopation. One of the most interesting features was the rhythmic excitement found in many of the works, both spiritual and otherwise, which typified African rhythms. The fast-slow note scheme and the syncopated effects were used frequently as in ♪♩ or ♫♫ and ♪♩♪ while other rhythms were strict, straightforward and hymn-like in appearance and sound, such as in the first movement theme of the piano suite, *Scuppernong*.

Ex. 37. *Scuppernong,* Work. Copyright 1951, Templeton Publishing Co., Inc. International Copyright Secured. All Rights Reserved. Sole Selling Agent: Shawnee Press, Inc., Delaware Gap, Pa. 18327.

Fig. 14. John W. Work III. Courtesy of Fisk University.

Not all of John Work's music was strictly romantic and homophonic. Some melodic overlapping, as well as open harmonies and mild dissonances were also used. *Soliloquy,* one of his vocal art songs, displayed a more modern background of harmony and style.

Ex. 38. *Soliloquy,* Work. Copyright © 1946 by Galaxy Music Corporation. All Rights Reserved. Used by permission.

Recently, his works were presented to the Fisk Library, the Special Collections. Among the approximately 113 compositions were: *Appalachia for Piano; Cazonet for Humming Chorus; American Negro Songs and Spirituals* (collection of 221 religious and secular examples); *Nocturne* (3 pieces for violin and piano); *Variations on an Original Theme* (piano); *Family Album* (5 piano pieces); *Golgotha is a Mountain* for 4 soloists and mixed voices, poem by Arna Bontemps); *Taliafero* (concert overture for Symphony orchestra); *Danse Africaine* (mixed voices, piano, drum, triangle; poem by Langston Hughes); *Do Not I Love Thee, O My Lord; Dusk at Sea* (art song); *Give me Jesus; Give me your Hand; All I Want; This Little Light O' Mine; Three Glimpses of Night; To a Mona Lisa; This Ol' Hammer!; T'was on One Sunday Morning; Unto the Hills I Lift Mine Eyes; You May Bury Me in the East; When Your Lamp Burns Down; Wasn't that a Mighty Day?; Little Black Train; Lord of All Being; Mandy Lou; Soliloquy* (solo voice and piano); *Sasafras* (piano); *Sing, O Heavens; Sinner Man, You Need Jesus; Isaac Watts contemplates the Cross; Night in La Vallee* (2 pianos) and others.

110

UNDINE SMITH MOORE (1904-   )

Undine Moore, a composer, arranger, pianist, organist, lecturer and educator, was born in Jarrat, Virginia, before assuming her permanent residence in Petersburg, Virginia. Educated at Fisk University where she graduated with honors as the highest ranking student in her class, she also studied at the Juilliard School of Music, Columbia University and the Eastman School of Music. Among her various teachers was Howard Murphy with whom she studied theory.

For her exceptional work as a teacher of students (which included Camilla Williams and Billy Taylor) Virginia State College awarded Mrs. Moore an honorary doctorate upon her retirement as co-director of the Black Music Center. Undine Moore is now visiting lecturer at several colleges, including Carleton College in Northfield, Minnesota. In demand as guest lecturer on music by Black composers, her lectures and workshops have been given at such institutions as Howard University, Fisk University and Indiana University. Her professional experiences have also included those of supervisor of music in Goldsboro, North Carolina, and theorist and lecturer at Virginia State's Department of Music.

Undine Moore's commissioned compositions have been heard at innumerable concerts such as the Fisk University Spring Festival of Music and the Fisk Jubilee Day celebration, Indiana University's Festival of Black Music, and recently, at Town Hall in New York City, where her former students sponsored a tribute of her original works in concert. Although her compositions are generally of a clear, concise, tonal style, two of her most recent works, the *Afro-American Suite* (commissioned by Trio Pro Viva) and the *Three Pieces for Flute and Piano,* have gradually expanded into more dissonant concepts of modern harmonies such as block chords or clusters and twelve-tone assimilations, respectively. Of homophonic and polyphonic textures, her structures are well formed and full of emotional sensitivity and change.

Among her works are: *Afro-American Suite for Flute, Cello and Piano; Lord, We Give Thanks to Thee for These Thy Servants; Mother to Son; Hail Warrior; Daniel, Daniel, Servant of the Lord; Let Us Make Man in Our Image; Striving After God; The Lamb; Long Fare You Well; Bound for Canaan's Land; Just Come from the Fountain; A Christmas Alleluia;* and others.

MARGARET BOND (1913-1972)

Margaret Bond, composer, author, conductor and pianist, was born in Chicago. She was educated at Northwestern University, where she received the B.M. and M.M. degrees, and the Juilliard School of Music. She also studied with Roy Harris, Emerson Harper, Robert Starer, William Dawson and Florence Price, and received awards from the National Association of Negro Musicians, the Alpha Kappa Alpha Sorority, the Julius Rosenwald Foundation, Roy Harris and the Wanamaker Award.

An accomplished pianist, Margaret Bond appeared innumerable times

Fig. 15. Undine Smith Moore.

in concerts, engaged in the accompanying of many vocal artists (one of which was Abbie Mitchell), and also used her skills to good advantage in the performance of her own compositions for piano. In the *International Library of Negro Life and History,* she is pictured as guest soloist with the Women's Symphony Orchestra in 1934, where she performed Florence Price's *Concerto in F Minor.*

As a composer, Margaret Bond was known for her countless arrangements of spirituals, her piano works and other orchestral and vocal compositions, both dramatic and abstract. Because she taught at the American Theater Wing, served as musical director of the Stage for Youth, the East Side Settlement House, and the White Barn Theater, she was well experienced in work for the stage. Such compositions as her *Shakespeare in Harlem* and *USA* are representative of her dramatic works. With her instinct for culture, she directed her efforts in promoting topics and techniques of the Black American. Such collaborators as Countee Cullen, Langston Hughes and others were instrumental in the strengthening of such works as her *The Negro Speaks of Rivers.* Both her productivity and the ideas used in her works have been far-reaching and commendable.

Much of Bond's established compositions were representative of the Romantic style. Others used idioms of the modern era. Having tested her ideas in various media without restricting herself to vocal music alone, she demonstrated certain natural writing she herself described as being a mixture of Marion Cook, H. T. Burleigh and Tchaikovsky. Her works show "jazzy" chords, both altered and augmented. The featured sevenths in clusters and widely spaced intervals and a jumping, rag-time bass, imitation and syncopations all reflect her style. In her *Ballad of a Brown King,* the combination of drama and music show a skill characteristic of a sound musician. In her spiritual arrangement of *I Got a Home in that Rock,* another style of writing is shown where syncopation and jazz chords border on ragtime.

Among Bond's compositions are: *The Negro Speaks of Rivers; Three Dream Portraits; Peter and the Bells; Mass in D; Troubled Island; Empty Interlude; Peachtree Street; Spring Will be so Sad; Fields of Wonder; Dry Bones; Lord I Just Can't Keep from Crying; I'll Reach to Heaven; Sit Down Servant; Suite for Piano; Music for Voice and Piano; He's Got the Whole World in His Hands.*

MITCHELL SOUTHALL (1922-   )

Mitchell Southall, a composer, arranger, conductor and educator, was born in Rochester, New York. Currently residing in Ita Bena, Mississippi, he serves as theorist-conductor at Mississippi Valley State College.

Dr. Southall was educated at Langston University, the University of Iowa and at the Oklahoma College of Liberal Arts. His experiences have won him several listings in *Who's Who In Music* as well as other awards given him by universities and associations. He has appeared as both classical pianist and guest conductor at many concerts, choral festivals and on radio and television broadcasts; he has also conducted and performed jazz at night clubs and institutions, for which he has been praised by *Down Beat* magazine.

His compositions have enjoyed equal success in performance, having been used at festivals and other concerts throughout the United States. Of a tonal style, these works range from homophonic to slight overlapping in harmonic and melodic interplay. His arrangements of spirituals such as *Sometimes I Feel Like a Motherless Child* are consistent with modern rhythmic features including syncopation and slight deviations from the traditional framework. Yet the ever-changing metric pulses flow easily with the familiar melodies, altered chords and concrete form.

His works also include: *Romance* for Piano; *Elf Dance; Impromptu; In Silent Night* for mixed chorus; *Piano Concerto;* numerous spiritual arrangements for choral ensemble; *Lady Be Good* for male voices; *Intermezzo;* and *De Lawd God A'Mighty's On His Throne.*

Modern Composers

Black composers of modern music are participants in techniques involving establishments of the Impressionistic era and the early 1900's. Characteristics of Debussy and Ravel as well as Charles Ives, Erik Satie, Poulenc and jazz set the stage for parallelism, block chords, polytonality, polyrhythms, longer melodic lines versus sporadic melodies, extended chords and ultra-chromatic harmonies, as well as the use of atonalism or the abandonment of a tonal center. Composers now use pentatonic or other modal harmonies intertwined with elements of the Baroque and earlier periods in order to denote a "new" sound and approach.

The modern period of the twentieth century denotes the machine and space ages, and is typified by the intervallic, instrumental approach rather than the vocal. The music is considered more impersonal and void of exaggerated emotional characteristics, and is an attempt to express the freedom of all emotions with restraint and perfect moderation.

WILLIAM GRANT STILL (1895-   )

William Grant Still, a legendary giant of American composers, was born in Woodville, Mississippi. Partially reared in Arkansas, Grant now resides in Los Angeles, California, where he still pursues his love for music daily.

Still was educated in Arkansas, at Wilberforce University, Oberlin Conservatory, and the New England Conservatory. A winner of many awards, Still excelled in composition which brought him the Guggenheim and Rosenwald Fellowships. In 1955, Still became the first Black to conduct a major symphony orchestra in the deep South when he directed the New Orleans Philharmonic in two of his own works. In addition to the New Orleans Philharmonic, he has conducted the Los Angeles Philharmonic at the Hollywood Bowl.

Other honors have been awarded the composer-conductor in the form of commissions from the Columbia Broadcasting System, the New York

114

Fig. 16. William Grant Still.

World's Fair, Paul Whiteman, the League of Composers and the Cleveland Orchestra. The Cincinnati Symphony Orchestra awarded him a prize in 1944 for the writing of an overture in celebration of its jubilee season. He also won the Harmon Award in 1928; a trophy from Local 767 of the Musicians' Union was also given, and honorary degrees have been awarded him from Wilberforce University (M.M.), Howard University (Mus. D.) and from Bates College (Doctor of Letters).

Still began the study of music under the encouragement of his mother. However, she warned him of the difficulty of many fine musicians who were not invited to the best of homes (as was the case of the early jazz and minstrel composers) but did not prevent his musical career. He was instructed on the violin at an early age, and his compositional traits showed a reflection of this training. Still also came under the strong influence of his teacher, Edgar Varèse.

Having composed in virtually all major forms and media from popular to classical, his thorough knowledge of orchestration, keyboard and vocal capacities are well known. Reviews, newspapers and other printed media related his accomplishments:

One of our greatest American composers. He has made a real contribution to music.   —Stokowski, 1945

This American composer shows remarkable qualifications which place him as one of the very greatest living composers of the New World; a sense of immediate observation; the taste for a rigorous and brilliant orchestration; spontaneity and sincerity characterize his compositions.   —*Micro Magazine,* 1955

This is real music, music of a composer of exotic talent and temperament, who has a keen sense of beauty and sensuousness which is controlled by taste . . . and unquestionable gift and warm feeling, now sad, now gay, characteristic and sincere in expression . . . increasing mastery on the part of the composer . . .
—*New York Times*

In his piano suite, *Bells,* the movements *Phantom Chapel* and *Fairy Knoll* were derived from an impressionistic period of obscurred harmonies. Measures 27-30 (*Phantom*) and 67-70 (*Fairy*) are given:

Ex. 39.   *Phantom Chapel,* Still. © Copyright 1944 by MCA Music, A Division of MCA, Inc., 445 Park Avenue, New York, New York 10022. Used by permission. All rights reserved.

Still's *Afro-American Symphony* earned the respect, inspiration and interest of younger composers. Based on themes derived from the blues, spirituals, jazz elements and familiar devices to the populace, Still integrated two worlds of music through quality writing and adaptation. This work became popular around 1933 and has been performed many times. His *Little Song That Wanted to be a Symphony* has been compared to Prokofieff's *Peter and the Wolf* in design. He also composed operas, choral works and various other smaller forms.

Some of Still's works show fragmentary phrases and tremolo devices as in measures five and seven (piano introduction) of his *Plain-Chant for America,* a piece for baritone solo with piano accompaniment. Perhaps the highlight of the piece is its message of measures 99-104, Ex. 40.

Ex. 40. *Plain-Chant for America,* Still. Copyright by William G. Still. Used by permission.

Still's opera, *Highway No. 1,* was recently included in the repertoire of Opera South, Jackson, Mississippi (libretto by his wife, Verna Arvey). Another of his operas, *Troubled Island,* referred to the Island of Haiti where revolt and everyday events were represented by motivic themes.

Among the extraordinarily extensive list of Still's works are: *In Memoriam: The Negro Soldiers Who Died for Democracy; Songs of a New Race; From the Black Belt; Lenox Avenue* (ballet); *Troubled Island* (opera, lyrics by Langston Hughes); *Mota; La Guiablesse* (ballet); *Sahjdi; And They Hanged Him on a Tree; Songs of Separation; Suite for Violin; From the Delta; Highway 1, USA; Miss Sally's Party* (ballet); *In Memory of Jan Sibelius; Little Song that Wanted to be a Symphony; Afro-American Symphony; Every Time I Feel the Spirit; Poem for Orchestra; Three Visions* (piano); *Seven Traceries* (piano); *Bells* (two pieces for piano; *Phantom Chapel* and *Fairy Knoll*); *Danzas de Panama* (string quarter); *Miniatures; Vignettes; Folk Suites Nos. 1, 2, 3; Winter's Approach* (voice and piano) *From the Lost Continent* (chorus); *Plåin Chant for America* (voice and orchestra); *From the Delta* (band); *Darker American* (orchestra); *Suite* (violin, *African Dancer,* etc.); *Those Who Wait; Here's One; A Deserted Plantation; Five Animal Sketches* (piano); and other spirituals and original compositions.

117

Howard Swanson, a composer who was born in Atlanta, Georgia, and reared in Cleveland, is now a resident of New York. He attended the Cleveland Institute of Music, and later won the Rosenwald Fellowship which sent him to Europe for study with Nadia Boulanger of Paris. Swanson also studied with Elwell and was influenced by the Romantic and Modern styles.

Swanson achieved fame through his songs, some of which were performed by Marian Anderson. His *Short Symphony,* written in 1948, was judged the best work of the season by the New York Music Critics Circle in 1952, and the same piece was performed in 1950 with Mitropoulos as conductor of the New York Philharmonic Orchestra. His art songs *I've Known Rivers* and *Joy* were widely used as effective concert pieces.

Swanson's style of writing varies from the Romantic to the Modern. His compositions also depict well planned melodies of long or short durations, sound balance between melody and accompaniment of piano versus vocal solo, or violins versus orchestral background. While the art song *Joy* uses mainly consonances and virtuosic techniques for both voice and piano, the orchestral piece, *Night Music,* employs more dissonance and polyphony of the modern period.

Among his works written are numerous songs and arrangements: *Short Symphony; Symphony No. 1; Night Music* (for small orchestra, woodwinds, horn, and strings) *Suite for Cello and Piano; Sound Piece for Brass Quintet; The Cuckoo* (piano scherzo); *Music for Strings; Seven Songs for Voice and Piano; Piano Sonata; Death Song; Cahoots;* and others.

MARK FAX (1911-   )
Mark Fax, composer, educator and director of the Department of Music at Howard University, was born in Baltimore, Maryland. Educated at Syracuse University and the Eastman School of Music, he has been awarded numerous honors and awards for his compositions and general contributions to music.

Fax has used both Romantic and Modern styles in writing, as well as contemporary techniques which lean toward atonality. His works are well organized, well balanced and challenging to perform. Intervals of seconds, fourths, fifths, or the use of altered chords and chromatics are pitted against clear, concise lines of sixteenth notes or sustained, smooth melodies. Many of the patterns of both harmonies and irregular intervals are so intricately constructed that the impression of atonalism is predominately felt. Yet a mixture of both tonal and atonal features are used in his works, with unusual skips in the upper and lower registers, trills and difficult rhythms. This style is reflected in *Toccata* from *Three Pieces for Piano,* the first measures of which are seen in Example 41:

Ex. 41. *Toccata* from *Three Pieces for Piano,* Fax. Used by permission of the composer.

Fax's compositions are for orchestral, chamber, vocal and other media, and include art songs, arrangements, opera, piano and organ pieces. Some of these works are entitled *Three Organ Pieces, Three Piano Pieces, Longing, May Day Song,* and *Only Dreams.*

NOAH RYDER (1914-1964)

Noah Ryder was a composer, educator and theorist who was born in Nashville, Tennessee. Ryder died in Norfolk, Virginia, where he had taught for several years. Educated at Hampton Institute (B.S.) and the University of Michigan (M.M.), his career before his Norfolk settlement took him to North Carolina where he had served as music supervisor at Goldsboro during 1935-1936. He served at the Palmer Institute at Sadalia as director from 1936-1938, and at Teachers College from 1938-1941 (Winston-Salem).

Ryder later became conductor of the Choir at Hampton and head of the theory department during 1941-44. He then was director of the Department of Music at the Norfolk Division of Virginia State College. Simultaneously, he directed the Harry Burleigh Glee Clubs of Virginia, and served as adjudicator for Omega Talent Hunts and various public school and institutional contests.

Ryder composed for various media, the most famous of which were his vocal songs. Arranged for solo voice and chorus, he wrote spirituals and art songs which used both traditional harmonies and modern techniques. His style of writing showed an advanced mastery of his art as well as genuine feel for the media for which he composed.

His piano work, *Idyll,* was written in 6/4 meter and incorporated an effect of a barless measure in its phrasing of "three". Arranged in legato intervals of fifths, the melodic implication was fresh in its similar motion. Ryder's *Rhapsodie* was reflective of both Rachmaninoff and Bartok. By using extremities of the keyboard, pedal points effecting obscure harmonies, and frequent metric changes from 4/4 to 2/4, he developed interesting effects. The use of three measure phrases rather than the traditional four; the triplet figures in quarters (♩♩♩), and continuous parallelism were equally interesting features of his music.

Among Ryder's varied compositions were: *Idyll* (piano) *Rhapsodie* (piano); *Serenade* (piano); *Sea Suite* (male voices); *Haul Away, Mateys, We're Almost Home* (Navy War Winter's Prize); *Balm in Gilead; By an' By; Done Paid My Vow; Let Us Break Bread Together; Gonna Journey*

119

Away; Great Day; Gwine Up; Hear the Lambs A'crying; I Got a Mother in Heaven; I Heard the Preaching of the Elders; I Will Never Betray My Lord; Nobody Knows; O Lemme Shine; Run to Jesus; and other songs for solo, chorus, etc.

THOMAS KERR (1915-   )

Thomas Kerr, a native of Baltimore, Maryland, now resides in Washington, D.C. Having received three degrees as a scholarship and fellowship student at the Eastman School of Music, he also studied at Howard University for a brief period of time. Ultimately, he was invited to Howard University School of Music where he is now full professor and chairman of the piano department.

Kerr has been awarded prizes in composition from the Composers and Authors of America Contest in 1941 to the Rosenwald Fellowship. Recitals of his organ works have been performed in the United States and Europe, at the Washington Cathedral, the Shrine of Immaculate Conception, Mormon Tabernacle and the Martin Luther King broadcast on Voice of America of 1971. Others of his works have been performed at various institutions and on recordings. His honors have also included his numerous piano appearances with the National Symphony Orchestra, at the National Gallery, Phillip's Gallery and at many universities throughout the United States.

Kerr writes in both tonal and atonal styles of the twentieth century. His ability to use clusters or blocks of sounds as well as simple homophony or mild polyphony is evident. His rhythmic patterns are exciting, and he is able to deal with short or long melodies with equal charm, using themes from original or folk sources.

Among his compositions are: *Caprice for Piano; Organic Metamorphoses on an Afro-American Melody; Filets of Soul for Woodwind Quartet; Anguished American Easter; Easter Monday Swagger, Scherzino; Arietta; Seven Dancetudes for Piano; Fanfares for Christmas* (chorus); *Three Dunbar Songs; Centennial Anthem* for Large Chorus, brass and organ; *Prayer for the Peace of the Soul of Martin Luther King* (chorus); and others.

ULYSSES SIMPSON KAY (1917-   )

Ulysses Kay, currently a composer and music consultant for Broadcast Music Inc., in New York, was born in Tucson, Arizona. Graduated from the University of Arizona, Kay also attended the Eastman School of Music in Rochester (M.A.), the Berkshire Music Center and Yale University. His teacher of composition was Paul Hindemith.

A recipient of many awards and honors, Kay was granted a Ditson Fellowship for creative work at Columbia University; the Julius Rosenwald Fellowship; a Prix de Rome for residence at the American Academy in Rome for the seasons 1949-1950 and 1951-1952; a Fulbright Scholarship to Italy in 1950-1951; a grant from the American Academy of Arts and Letters; and a grant from the National Institute of Arts and Letters. Other

Fig. 17. Ulysses Kay.

prizes have been awarded for several of his works, including *Suite for Orchestra, A Short Overture* and *Of New Horizons*. Recently, Kay was awarded a Guggenheim Fellowship and honorary doctorates from Lincoln College and Bucknell University.

A well established composer of note, Kay has composed various compositions from popular to art music. Commissions have come from the Cornell University, A Cappella Choir; the Greater Boston Youth Symphony; Illinois Wesleyan Collegiate Choir; Interracial Fellowship Chorus of New York; the Koussevitzky Music Foundation and others.

Kay has been to the Soviet Union as a member of the first group of American composers sent on a cultural exchange mission by the State

121

Department. His distinguished career has also involved composing scores for films and television. In addition, Kay has lectured at Boston University, the University of California at Los Angeles, and currently serves as Professor of Music at the Herbert H. Lehman College of the City University of New York.

Of his music, Howard Klein of the New York Times has said: "Mr. Kay calls himself a traditionalist — an evasive term. But his music is tonal and very direct. It comes out of romantic and expressionist chromatic styles of this century . . ." Also described as rhapsodic, melodic, classical and modern, Kay's works invite analysis relating it to many periods. He is very representative of the contemporary era.

Even though a good many of Kay's works are of the neo-Baroque tradition in contrapuntal features and forms, much of that which has gone before reflects the classical period in form. His latest works such as *Parables* show a decided change in the intervallic concept of the contemporary period. Seconds, fourths, sevenths, etc., always characterized his music, as did rhythms typical of the contemporary period. Kay is significant for linking the Modern Period with the Space Age in his forward use of contemporary techniques, much as did Beethoven who bridged the classical and Romantic periods. Kay is one who produces quality works, and his courageous approach of maintaining a traditional principle amidst irregular, or contemporary methods, is unique.

One of the examples of his works is the *Four Inventions* for piano. An advanced compositional technique of fugal or imitative features, it uses twelve tone principles fused with tonalism, and generally obscures the key while functioning within a harmonic structure. Written in four movements: Andante moderato, Scherzando, Larghetto, and Allegro, the movements are scored without a key signature but do not always remain in C Major. The first movement ends on G minor; the second on A minor (without a third); the third on Ab major; and the fourth in C major. Slightly vocal, the piece, particularly in the first movement, sounds atonal despite its movement within G minor chord progressions. This results from a rhythm which places chord tones an eighth note apart from other chord tones, while the melody accents the dissonance. Nevertheless, the first movement does use all the notes of the G minor chord both in the first and last measures, thus confirming a tonal center:

Ex. 42. *Four Inventions,* Kay. © Copyright, 1964, Duchess Music Corporation, 445 Park Avenue, New York, New York 10022. Used by permission. All rights reserved.

The second movement (Ex. 43), given in 5/8, outlines irregular phrasing at the beginning. In its unique expression, inverted mordents, incomplete scale passages and short phrases are typical. It terminates in extreme registers, and makes use of wide intervals within the melodic lines:

Ex. 43. Second Movement.

The third movement makes use of accidentals which are written in, and jazz harmonies of elongated sevenths, ninths or polychords. Typical rhythmic changes alternate between 4/8 and 6/8 in its somewhat sectional character. Melodies shift from bass to treble in the exchange of the main subject. Dynamic extremes and the use of three clefs are also used. The main subject is seen in Example 44.

Ex. 44. Third Movement, main subject.

The last movement, a two-part invention, is the most difficult of the four. Even though written in 4/4, its accented staccatos and breaks slurred meticulously throughout make it a challenge to perform. Scales in contrary motion, unexpected metric changes, and variations in dynamics bring the work to a close:

Ex. 45. Fourth Movement.

123

While the above examples exhibit his piano technique, Kay is equally noted for his quality of style in orchestral and other music. Although his long list of works include music for virtually all media, the great majority of compositions are written for the orchestra and for chorus. His *Umbrian Scene* has been performed by the Louisville Symphony Orchestra. The *Serenade for Orchestra* has been performed by the Chicago Symphony Orchestra. And his opera, *Juggler of Our Lady,* was recently included in the repertoire of Opera South, of Jackson, Mississippi. With keen sensitivity to taste in orchestral colors and combinations of sounds in general, Kay uses the extremes in high and low pitches with unusual dissonance.

Ancient Saga, a design for modern dance, was written in 1947. Scored for piano, three violins, violas, cello and contrabass, it includes parallelism, polymeters, many key and tempo changes and interesting rhythmic patterns. Measures 173-176, excerpted in Example 46, point out some of these features:

Ex. 46. *Ancient Saga,* Kay. © Copyright 1972 by Duchess Music Corporation, 445 Park Avenue, New York, New York 10022. Used by permission. All rights reserved.

Among his works are: *A Short Overture; Aulos; Concerto for Orchestra; Fantasy Variations; Markings; Overture; Of New Horizons; Portrait Suite; Orchestra; Symphony; Trigon; Umbrian Suite; Choral Triptych; Inscriptions from Whitman* (cantata for voice and orchestra); *Stephen Crane Set* (94 pieces for SATB and 13 players); *Three Pieces After Blake* (soprano and orchestra); *Six Dances; A Lincoln Letter; A New Song; How Stands the Glass Around?* (vocal); *Come Away, Come Away Death; Flowers in the Valley; Four Hymn-Anthems; Grace to You and Peace; Song of Jeremiah; Tears, Flow No More; What's in a Name?; Brass Quartet; Four Inventions* (piano); String Quartet Nos. 2, 3; *Trumpet Fan-Fares* (4 trumpets); *Ten Essays for Piano; Two Short Pieces for Piano* (4 hands); *The Boor* (opera); *The Juggler of Our Lady* (opera); and many others.

Black composers of art music showed talent, drive, skill and patience in their efforts, and a courage keenly related to the truth and freedom

124

sought in the subsequent contemporary era. They proved and conquered! They proved that they could indeed compose in any style chosen. The question of "stereotype" or the myth that Blacks could not be intellectual was weakened to the extent that all America could more readily relate to the idea of freedom in musical professionalism. This fact was true despite the laxity in the promotion of this music.

The fact that not all Blacks could compose jazz was realized. Not all Blacks wanted to do so! It was also a reality that many Blacks within art music used jazz techniques within the art music forms long before the third stream music was popularized in the 1960's. Whether or not these composers developed jazz or art music, however, is not as important as the fact of their contribution to American music, and their efforts to remove obstacles encountered by all Black musicians. For these composers were not so much involved in the definition of "true" Black music as they were in the struggle and right to pursue self-expression. They were as concerned with their identity as any musician, but were also involved in working within the established definitions of music.

PART THREE

FREEDOM NOW
(1950-1970)

XI
CONTEMPORARY PERIOD:
THE BLACK REVOLUTION

Black voices of the twentieth century coordinated a cultural, artistic and proud revolution during the era of the new Civil Rights struggle. Frustration from centuries of injustice and denial culminated in new campaigns for civil rights during the mid-1950's and the early 1960's. These activities began in the southern regions of the Country, moved to the north and throughout the Nation. Leaders from Martin Luther King and Malcolm X to Stokely Carmichael, Frantz Fanon and C. L. R. James urged demonstrations and confrontations which ultimately resulted in some changes in public and educational accommodations as well as some liberties of mind and morals. Civil rights struggles occurred before Reconstruction, and occurred thereafter, but never had they commanded the right to exist in so loud a voice as in the silence of the marches. The struggle for dignity and respect focused their attentions on the conscience of all America.

Then came a revolution of arts and ideas which served as a guide to worthwhile achievements and progress. Pan-Africanism had greatly spurred the challenge for the right to pursue happiness and freedom. There was much pride felt by Blacks in America in the recent independence won by African states. The colorful leaders of Africa and their new image caused Blacks to closely relate to those inhabitants of the Mother Country with renewed respect and brotherhood. A bitterness welled inside the hearts of those Black Americans who had not won in America an independence easily seen elsewhere. The loss of dignity and self-esteem and the loss of language and cultural norms were seen as an affront to human justice, and as a punishment for being Black. Blacks in America were determined to follow their African brothers.

Blacks were furthermore determined to overcome the barrier which spoke so stoically of the "status quo" in America. They sang a blues which reiterated their frustration: *I'm Tired of Bein' Jim Crowed.* They also fervently sang an old spiritual in march time, *Many Thousand Gone,* paraphrased to suit the new occasion of *We Shall Overcome.* This song showed the unity of spirit and mind and vowed not to become destined to the status of semi-slavery in 1960 as they had in 1619. This time, the Constitution had guaranteed the rights for which they struggled; this time, Black soldiers in Korea and Vietnam had defended American freedom. And this time,

129

they were aware of the heritage which produced advancements of civilizations, both old and new.

The Breakthrough

The direct confrontations with society ultimately led to the breakdown of some of the barriers of segregation during the 1960's. Simultaneous with these developments came the breakdown of barriers in the field of music. Perhaps this was the result of early pioneers of long ago; it could also have been the early acceptance of the vocalists, or the belated realization that Blacks could indulge in more areas than the art of singing. Nevertheless, unions generally changed their rules to admit a few Blacks, and performers and composers were gradually admitted into more levels of professional advancement than before. Significantly, a few players became members of symphony orchestras. The New World Symphony Orchestra was composed and organized for minorities. More opera stars were allowed to compete in higher levels of achievement, and Black conductors were slowly being accepted. Still, Black composers are hampered by both publishers who do not advertise extensively and recording industries who do not promote their works, but this era does indeed represent some promise of a greater degree of freedom in all aspects of Black life.

XII
NEW AFRICA: A CYCLIC RETURN

The fact of African independence was instrumental in setting the stage for the call to freedom, and for the Second Black Renaissance of to-day. Suddenly, Blacks from George Bridgetower and Samuel Coleridge-Taylor to Alexandre Dumas became increasingly important. From this came a swift and decided turn toward the sincere study of Black culture, from mores to music.

As America had borrowed from African music, particularly through Black sources, it now used those aspects of African music which it needed, and with full knowledge of the reasons why. The traditional African aspect of the music penetrated forms from jazz to art music.

America hastened to learn about the music of Africa. Many scholars followed the advice of African writers who urged that Africa itself had to become the center of learning. They traveled to Africa in order to partake of the traditional activities and resources which were present. Musicians in jazz and art music also studied African features intensely and encouraged the rapid acceptance and use of music. Western musicians once again reaffirmed the base from whence a part of western music was derived.

Many Blacks pursued a theory of Pan Africanism in relating music of all Blacks to that of Africa. It was important not only for the relationship of Black cultures, but for music in all such cultures. For some, the closer the link with older precepts the better the understanding and knowledge of musical origin became. Since many aspects of music were universal, Africa became speculative in the derivation of all music.

American institutions sought out musicologists and composers from Africa so that further interchange could begin in the study of African music. Teams of American composers were greatly interested in the music of traditional African composers. Among those whom they sought were Halim El-Dabh from Egypt, Fela Sowande from Nigeria and J. Kwabena Nketia from Ghana. All well trained and gifted musicians in both composition and historical research and performance, these musicians became the modern "griots" of the contemporary world who could relate to the musical tradition in Africa.

In addition to their being steeped in the practices and knowledge of African music, these composers were themselves ironically influenced by, and keenly aware of, western traditions in music. They had, like the Black Americans, composed in an African and a western style, and had sought to determine the truth of their own styles. Consequently, that which had be-

131

gun in Africa and moved to the west had now returned to influence once again. The primary source, Africa, had been replenished by generations of mutations, and had become new Africa, while America benefited as the keeper of the tradition.

EPHRAIM AMU (1899-   )

The Black pioneer of systematic West African research was Ephraim Amu who, when he returned from England as a stranger to his indigenous music, decided to devote his lifetime to the study, transcription and teaching of African music. Born in the Volta Region of Peki-Avetile, Ghana, he was educated at Peki, then the Training College of Basel Mission Seminary, Abelifi (Presbyterian Trinity, Akwapen-Akropong). Further training was done in London at the Royal College of Music. Among his honors was the honorary doctorate from the University of Ghana.

His teaching experience began in 1930 at the Bremen Mission (Evangelical Presbyterian Middle School, Peki-Blengo). He also taught at the Presbyterian Training College, Achimota College, the College of Art, Science and Technology at Kumasi, and served as Music Researcher at Kumasi Technology.

Amu currently works at the University of Ghana in Legon, having been invited as a Senior Research Fellow after his retirement from the University. In his spare time, he conducts his church choir in the singing of African music and carves Ghanaian musical instruments.

As a composer, teacher and performer, he has been instrumental in influencing other leading musicologists and African musicians to follow his example to study and preserve African music. Following the publication of his book, *Twenty-five African Songs,* serious scholars became interested in his concept of cultural preservation and research.

Amu shows a preference for the vocal medium, although he has composed for both western and African instruments. He also prefers the Twi language. In some of his music, African scales and harmonies prevail while western styles of major and minor tonalities with dynamics and other marks of interpretation appear. A piece entitled *Traditional Atentenbenj Prelude,* a duet for two wind players, contains clusters of ornaments common to early Baroque and polyphonic textures. The rhythms are characteristically African as shown:

Ex. 47.   *Atentenbenj Prelude,* Amu. Used by permission of African Institute, University of Ghana at Legon.

132

Fig. 18. Ephraim Amu.

Another of his pieces, *Wo Nsam Mewo* is written for male voices in tonal hymn style, excerpted in Example 48.

Ex. 48. *Wo Nsam Mewo*, Amu. Used by permission of African Institute, University of Ghana at Legon.

Among Amu's works are: *Adawura Bome; Three Solo Songs; Two Pieces for Bamboo Flute and Piano; Twenty Piped Pieces; Ten Vocal Pieces, Wo Nsam Mewo; Enne Ye Anigyeda;* over 100 songs, and one book entitled *Twenty Five African Songs* (1932), now out of print.

J. KWABENA NKETIA (1921-   )

J. Kwabena Nketia, the leading musicologist-composer of Ghana, serves as the director of the African Institute at the University of Ghana. Nketia was educated at the Teacher Training College, Akropong Akuapem; the School of Oriental and African Studies at the University of London; Trinity College of Music, London (B.A.); at Columbia University; the Juilliard School of Music and Northwestern University. Once a student of Amu, he was greatly influenced by that pioneer of Ghanaian research.

133

His scholarships and honors include citations from the Ghana government, Rockefeller Foundation and Ford Foundation scholarships as well as the Cowell Award. An active and capable teacher, performer and musicologist, he also directs the musical ensemble which accompanies the Ghana Dance Troupe, and frequently lectures at American Universities and other institutions abroad. His teaching experience also includes the Presbyterian Training School and a Research Fellow and eventual Professor at the University of Ghana, where he currently directs the African Institute. Nketia has also served as principal at the Presbyterian School.

In addition to his lectures and composing, Nketia has written over 100 articles and books on music. Some of his publications are: *African Music in Ghana; The Poetry of Drums; Drum Proverbs; The Development of Instrumental African Music in Ghana; Drums, Dance and Song; Traditional Music of the Ga People; The Hocket Technique in African Music; Folk Songs of Ghana; Drumming in Akan Communities of Ghana; The Artist in Contemporary Africa; The Challenge of Tradition* and many others.

Nketia's style of composing ranges from the African to western types. His scales are either modal or are major and minor. His pieces are generally traditional in chord structure and are primarily consonant. His intervals are generally traditional elements of African and western music; (i.e., seconds, thirds, fourths, fifths, and octaves). The rhythm is the exciting aspect of his writing in which the smoothly constructed melodies flow unhampered within irregularly organized measures. One of his best compositions, the *Suite for Flute and Piano,* consisting of seven movements in all, contains many of the elements discussed. The first and second movement themes are excerpted in Example 49 and are not as easy to perform as they appear.

Ex. 49. *Suite for Flute and Piano*, Nketia. Used by permission of the African Institute, University of Ghana at Legon.

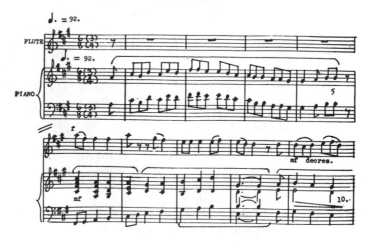

134

Fig. 19. J. Kwabena Nketia.　　Fig. 20. Ato Turkson.

Among Nketia's musical works are: *Four Akan Songs; Suite No. 1 for Flute and Piano; Four Flute Pieces; Canzona for Flute, Oboe, and Piano; Chamber Music in the African Idiom* (violin and piano w/Partos); *Eight Piano Pieces;* and other works.

ATO ALPHONSO TURKSON (1937-　　)

Ato Alphonso Turkson, a gifted young musician and composer of several works, has received his doctorate from Northwestern while on leave from the University of Ghana. He was educated at Achimoto College with Robert Kwamk, Philip Gbeho and J. Kwabena Nketia. He later accepted a composition fellowship to study in Hungary at the Franz Liszt Academy where he was a student of Kodaly's protégé, Rezso Sugar. His teaching experience was gained at the Winneba Secondary School and the University of Ghana, where he worked as a research assistant.

Turkson's works show a refreshing approach to composition in general, and is representative of the contemporary era. A mixture of the African-western style, his works sometimes use common scales but primarily utilize twelve tone techniques. The most Africanized aspect of his music is the rhythmic interest, an intricacy of cross-rhythms, sporadic fragments and extended lines.

His *Sonata for Violin and Piano,* Op 16, and the *Three Pieces for Flute and Piano* display a mastery of skill and a natural affinity for the characteristics of each instrument. Both challenging and well constructed, they demand talent and control. The first measures of *Three Pieces for Flute and Piano,* Op. 14 are shown in Example 50, taken from each of the three movements.

135

Ex. 50. *Three Pieces for Flute and Piano,* Op. 14, Turkson. Used by permission of the African Institute, University of Ghana at Legon.

HALIM EL-DABH (1921-   )

Halim El-Dabh was born and educated in Cairo, Egypt. He studied at Sulez Conservatory in Cairo from 1941-44. Graduating in agriculture, he later devoted full time to his music and by 1950 traveled to the United States. El-Dabh then attended New Mexico University, the New England Conservatory and Brandeis University. He studied with Irving Fine, Francis Cooke, and Aaron Copland. His teaching experience includes Howard University and Kent State University.

El-Dabh has composed well over 100 works for various media from African drums to the western piano. He has received prizes for his compositions. One such award was the Guggenheim Fellowship.

Of the African and western idioms, the music has not lost the flavor of his native Egypt. Seconds, clusters, octaves and unisons in simple com-

136

binations are placed against modal or tonal harmonies in short, rhythmic patterns.

El-Dabh has composed the following works: *Mekta in the Art of Kita;* books I-II; *Thulathiya* (trio for viola, oboe, and piano); *Juxtaposition No. 1* for two timpany, xylophone and marimba; *Twenty-five Arabiyaats* (arabic forms); *Misriyaats* (Egyptian forms); *Ifriqiyatts* (African forms); *Clythemnestra;* and various pieces for African and western instruments.

FELA SOWANDE (1905-   )

Fela Sowande was born in Nigeria, and is currently a teacher at Howard University. He was educated at the C. M. S. Grammar School and King's College in Lagos. Later, Sowande traveled to London where he studied as a Fellow of the Trinity College of Music (B. Mus.) and at the Royal College of Organists. He was taught by Oldroyd, Cunningham, Rubbra and others.

His experiences have included popular and art music. He led a dance band in London where he also became a recording artist for Decca Records. He has served as musical director to the Colonial Film Unit, provided background music for several educational films, and was organist and choirmaster to the West London Mission. He founded the Kingsway Musical Society and has directed the Yoruba Life Series in preserving indigenous music and folklore.

Sowande has also received various awards and honors. Among these have been the Rockefeller Foundation Grant, the Ford Foundation Grant and others. He has also served as guest conductor of the BBC Symphony Orchestra, as guest conductor of the New York Philharmonic, and the BBC Northern Orchestra. In Africa, he was a visiting Fellow and Member of the Advisory Council at the Hansberry College of African Studies, and the University of Ibadan in Nigeria, and was also Professor of Musicology at the University of Ibadan.

Other honors have included commissions for his works from the Nigerian Government for Independence Celebrations; the Nigerian Federal Ministry of Information for a special arrangement of the Nigerian National Anthem; and the Traditional Chieftaincy Award by the Lagos State, Federation of Nigeria, in recognition of research into Yoruba folklore.

The music of Sowande is based on both western and African techniques. Many of his actual themes are traditionally Nigerian such as the *Obangiji* which greatly resembles the Black spiritual, *Nobody Knows.* Significantly, Sowande has also used Black American spirituals as source materials. Sowande's concept of derivative materials is more representative of Pan Africanism than are the other African composers in that his subjects reflect both African and other universal themes of Black folk. His compositional substance generally outlines the Romantic and early Modern tradition. Some aspects of his music are emphasized in the rhythms seen in Example 51.

Ex. 51. Rhythms of Sowande.

Among Sowande's organ compositions are: *Kyrie* (based on a theme of Juti); *Yoruba Lament* (Nigerian theme); *Obangiji* (Nigerian theme); *Go Down Moses* (spiritual); *Joshua Fit de Battle; Jesu Olugabala; K'a Mura; Gloria* (based on a theme of Juti); *Oyigiyigi; and Prayer* (Nigerian theme). His vocal works include *Three Songs of Contemplation* for tenor; *Because of You for tenor; Sit Down Servant; The Gramercy of Sleep* (male choir); *Words* (males); *Sometimes I Feel Like a Motherless Child; My Way's Cloudy; De Ol' Ark's a Moverin'; Same Train; Steal Away; Roll de Chariot; All I Do; Goin' to Sit Down; Couldn't Hear Nobody Pray; Heav'n Bells are Ringin'; De Angels are Watchin'; Nobody Knows de Trouble I See; Wheel, Oh Wheel; Stan' Still Jordan;* and *Wid a Sword in Ma Han;* Sowande has also written *African Suite for Strings* (African themes) and *A Folk Symphony* (Nigerian themes) for full orchestra.

There are still more composers living in Africa who are not represented here. Notable among those missing is the Nigerian composer, Adam Fiberesima, whose opera, *Opu Jaja,* is currently being reviewed in Nigeria by Dr. Oscar Henry for performances at African and American Festivals of Arts and Culture. As Africa grows, such personalities will become as familiar as those known techniques which have been borrowed from Africa to make the music of America.

XIII
CONTEMPORARY JAZZ

Jazz of the contemporary era includes elements of "soul" blues and funky elements which penetrate gospel, rhythm and blues or rock and folk, as well as derivatives of its main style, "cool," "avant-garde" and "third stream." Jazz is yet influenced by European concepts but attempts to re-emphasize the African elements of music. During the present era of further experimentation with form, manner of performance and compositional materials, media from plastic and electrical timbres to those traditional are used, and there is a continual change based upon experiments culminating in the late fifties and early sixties which began in the 1940's.

In New York, "cool" jazz merged in the 1950's, overshadowing the popularity of "bop" and resembling the "progressive" punctuations in California. Practiced by Lester Young, Miles Davis and others, the styles were similar and emphasized the easy-going, the subdued and the relaxed. Cool jazz employed clear sounds, muted sounds, calmness, and yet a skillful technique and control. Also called "chamber jazz" because of its limited instrumentation, subdued sound and intellectual possibilities, melodic lines became extended in length and technical content of instrumental character. It also sponsored the addition of the flute, french horn, oboe, and English horn. Not particularly emotional, intense or over-active, "cool" utilized modern dissonances with traditional, close harmonic progressions, hazy sounds, obscurity of meters and abstractions akin to those of art music.

In quick reaction to "cool" came "hard bop," "soul" and "funky" styles of jazz which recaptured some of the earthy roots originally planted by the blues and older, influential forms. Polyrhythms, blocks or clusters and intricate accents continued along with the improvisational and other syncopated effects in order to direct jazz back to its original course. The complexities of styles already introduced within bop continued as exciting interrelated activities of small ensembles, soloists, and singers. Many of these latter types were also employed and originated by John Coltrane, Art Tatum, Bud Powell and Cannonball Adderley.

"Avant-garde" employs the freedom of self, an array of various improvisations, scales, arpeggios, leaps, and primarily melodic emphasis. With its influence of African, Asian and American elements, it also features modal as well as traditional western scale patterns. Yet the overall effect of the music is that of atonalism. Practiced and mainly promoted by Ornette Coleman and others, avant-garde boasts arbitrary and intricate procedures which have reaped quantities of both criticism and praise. The free interplay in collective ensemble may imply disorder to some, but to others, the freedom of expression in improvisation denotes the heart of jazz and a reflection of the era.

Third stream jazz, realized in the 1950's, involves the fusion of classical music and jazz in an ingenious compositional form which renders one almost inseparable from the other. Although jazz musicians had been previously influenced by art music, the similarity of technical devices and overall dignity of each form was never organized into structures as they exist today. The abstractions of both cool jazz and art music merges with the most sophisticated kinds of jazz to develop both tonal and atonal examples of third stream music. Like avant-garde and bop, third stream can either reflect its association with the blues or can relate to the simple homophony of a hymn. While cool and avant-garde may use instinct and spontaneity in performance, third stream is generally pre-constructed and generally outlines the period of improvisation as opposed to structured form.

Composers

The composers of the most recent jazz trends have joined in massive efforts to define, penetrate and reveal the nature and function of jazz. Their philosophies have become as important as their techniques for composition and are typical of the struggle for freedom and identity within the society. Spectacular timbres and emotions are decidedly representative of the era which these composers are attempting to portray. Representative persons of each style common to jazz are discussed in the order of their successive eras.

MILES DAVIS (1926-   )

Miles Davis, composer-trumpeter and arranger, was born in Illinois. He later moved to St. Louis, and eventually to New York, where he studied at the Juilliard School of Music. Highly influenced by Charlie Parker, Miles studied with Parker while attending Juilliard and expanded greatly during their association.

Miles organized a band for recording in 1948, headed several quintets and sextets, and performed both in the United States and abroad. He worked with Gil Evans, pianist; Max Roach, composer-drummer; Bud Powell; and John Coltrane. Since the later forties, his growth and performance abilities in concerts, recordings and films have created a popular following.

Miles developed several styles before he settled into a lyrical, sustained and introspective manner of composition. The long, extended lines of ornamental quality or the short, fragmented melodies flow over polychordal, sometimes atonal harmonies, orchestrated in either ballad style or in free, fantasy-like compositions. His rhythms move but are not considered swift. Intervals range from chromatics to wide varieties of skips and non-chordal tones, and the overall technique, though serene, is difficult to produce. He also experiments with various schemes for blues.

Among Davis' works are: *Deception; Sipping at the Bells; Oles;*

Dewey Square; The Theme; So What; Blue n' Boogie; Walkin'; Little Leaps; Sid's Ahead; Weirdo; Budo; Move; Venus de Milo; and others.

JOHN COLTRANE (1926-1967)

John Coltrane, a composer-saxophonist, was a jazz artist of many styles from traditional jazz to hard bop, and was also influential in establishing procedures and experiments toward avant-garde. Coltrane worked in New York and on several concert tours with Miles Davis and Thelonius Monk, whose intensive styles also helped mold Coltrane's own manner of playing and composing. In addition, Coltrane's principles of approach and familiarity with the saxophone were reflective of Coleman Hawkins. Some aspects can be heard in his recordings: *A Love Supreme; Duke Ellington w/Coltrane* and *Coltrane w/Johnny Hartman.*

A leading figure during his short lifetime, his works consisted of wide ranges of pleasant instrumental sounds to those of harsh qualities. His approach was ultimately from a lyrical standpoint, and melodically interpolated around harmony. With a highly ornamental melody as his predominant characteristic, complete dissonant tones would be employed with the harmony. Even though Coltrane used tonal actions in some compositions, many of his late works were atonal in quality, particularly because of the urgent, breathless and ornamental extensions of cadences.

Coltrane used western scales as well as modal characteristics of Asian and African scales. As one deeply interested in the identity of self, he used other characteristics of African derivatives. Improvisation, complex rhythms and the overlapping of rhythmic patterns were fused with the mixtures of scales and emotions. Partly under the influence of hard bop traditions of blues and other roots, his style also contained many elements of sharp intensity. Other explorations, however, were almost devoid of this fiery tradition of self and soul. Besides the blues form which he extended into different formal patterns of measures and meters, Coltrane used traditional ballads and free forms.

Much of his exploratory features were not conducive to relaxation but this became increasingly true of many contemporary jazz forms. Because of the many intricate sounds and rhythms created, one was forced to listen and sort the material presented in quite different ways than in the case of swing or other earlier music. For example, a simple fragment improvised innumerable ways, or the large amount of notes within a single phrase in either tonal or atonal patterns were presented along with extensions of vocal and instrumental timbres to include screams, grunts, and squeaks. There were rapidly repeated tones in complex multi-rhythmic frames, or "sputterings" of tones chromatically or diatonically styled as if unrelated to each other. The functions of harmony were contrary to the usual procedure, and the use of block chords and altered chords suggested by his lines were not always captured or readily comprehended by the listener. However, his music was exciting, difficult and demanding but representative of the times in which he lived.

141

Among his works arranged and composed were: *My Favorite Things; A Love Supreme; Suite; Transition; Chasin' the Trane; Take the Coltrane; How High the Moon; Impressions; Ascension; Crescent; Double Clutching; Summertime; But Not for Me; Shifting Down;* and others.

ORNETTE COLEMAN (1930-   )

Ornette Coleman, composer and saxophone player, is credited with much of the freedom of expression which contributed to contemporary jazz. Of the "avant-garde" school, his experiments have matured into a focus of the newest musical form. Born in Fort Worth, Texas, Coleman traveled extensively, and settled in New York. Having performed with numerous bands, he formed his own group on his return to Forth Worth. From carnivals in Fort Worth to tours and concerts elsewhere, he has gained in both experience and professionalism. At first mainly self-taught through instruction manuals, Coleman was influenced by John Lewis to attend the School of Jazz at Lenox, Massachusetts. Before that, he was influenced by Charlie Parker, Lester Young and James Jordan.

Most of Coleman's music is highly improvised, melodically conceived, and atonal. *His Circle with a Hole in the Middle,* recorded on his *Art of the Improvisers* album, is representative of his latest style. He is quoted by Ostermann in the National Observer of June 7, 1965, as having described the aspects of his avant-garde music: "I don't know how it's going to sound before I play it any more than anybody else does." With conventional or plastic timbres that imitate the human voice, he makes his way across a continent of emotions and techniques of scales and arpeggios. Chromatics and complex rhythms are typical of the music.

Among his compositions are: *Lonely Woman; Antiques; Broadway Blues; Round Trip; Sadness; Free Jazz; Complete Communion; Mapa; Ramblin'; Cross Breeding; Snowflakes and Sunshine; Dawn; Turn-Around; Congeniality; Focus on Sanity; Peace; Sphinx; Chippie; Something Else; Circle with a Hole in the Middle;* and others.

JOHN LEWIS (1920-   )

John Lewis, composer, arranger, music director and pianist, was born in LaGrange, Illinois, and settled in New York. With Milt Jackson, he formed the Modern Jazz Quartet and became known for quality music. A teacher at the Manhattan School of Music, Lewis was educated at the University of Mexico in both anthropology and music, and at the Manhattan School.

Influenced by Dizzy Gillespie, Charlie Parker and others, his own style also reflects those masters of the past: Bach, Haydn, Mozart, and Beethoven. This is apparent in his fugues, rondos and episodes which he fuses with third stream jazz fundamentals in various classical situations. Having once worked with Gillespie as arranger and pianist, their exchange of ideas merged with his own concepts.

Specializing in chamber jazz groups, Lewis has recorded with the

Modern Jazz Quartet and with Asmussen, the European jazz violinist. His music reflects the "progressive" features, the "cool" tendency and the aloofness and sensitivity of "bop." His music also represents organization, keen development and direction, for his thorough training lends to the music a sophistication which it might not otherwise have had to distinguish it from any other composition of traditional jazz. Certain of his compositions are written as though improvised, while others employ other substantial and clear organization. Much of his inspiration comes from the blues to which he reportedly feels a kinship. His penetrating style promotes a creative rhythmic certainty and a feel for jazz.

Among his compositions are: *Smoke Gets in Your Eyes; Delaunay's Dilemma; Two Bass Hit; Emanon; Stay on it; Sait-on Jamais; Exposure* (film score); *Odds Against Tomorrow* (film score); *Django* (guitar); *Jazz Quartet; Vendome; Versaillers; Concorde; The Queen's Fancy; Move; Budo; Rogue; Love Me; Three Little Feelings; Bluesology; Festival Sketch; Two Degrees East; Three Degrees West; The Golden Striker;* and others.

OLIVER NELSON (1933-   )

Oliver Nelson, a Pulitzer Prize winner, conductor, arranger, composer and saxophone player was born in Saint Louis and now lives in Los Angeles. Having once lived in New York, Oliver Nelson has made the rounds as a performer in all types of combos from those of the Temptations, Jimmy Rushing, Ray Charles and Sonny Rollins to Cannonball Adderly.

Educated privately at an early age, Nelson developed an interest in conducting after hearing Duke Ellington, Ravel and Hindemith. He has been influenced by others with whom he has worked, such as Count Basie and Quincy Jones. Yet his more advanced education has prepared him for both traditional jazz as well as for his own independence with the concepts of third stream and classical music.

Educated further at Washington University with Elliot Carter, Robert Wykes, and George Tremblay, Nelson has many credits to his name: *More Blues* and *the Abstract Truth* have won the 1965 Edison Award in Amsterdam; *The Kennedy Dream* has won the Deutsche Grammophone Award for 1967; *The American Wind Symphony* has presented a "Tribute to Oliver Nelson" when some of his classical and jazz pieces were performed and he has served as lecturer at universities (including Washington University where his composition, *Piece for Orchestra,* was premiered in 1969). Nelson also won the 12th International Jazz Critics Poll which was held by *Down Beat* magazine, and has been well reviewed in an outstanding tribute by *Ebony.*

His talents have also served to keep him in demand both as a lecturer and performer, in addition to his conducting and composing. He also conducts series of classes at various institutions. His recordings number about 20. Nelson has also arranged for Nancy Wilson, Brook Benton, Jimmy Smith, and others. Nelson has written a textbook on the improvisation of

143

jazz, and is capable of writing works from symphonies to blues. Even though he is aware of Classical art music, Nelson's own style dictates compositions within any type of music and for various media, without restriction and without reservations, from blues and gospels to orchestral pieces.

The music employs tonalities of traditional and contemporary types, meters in duple and triple time, and call and answer patterns of melody versus chords. Even though lyrical, the compositions nevertheless employ independence of line and harmonic patterns, and move in improvised and planned structures. Equally and keenly aware of instrumental and vocal characteristics, the music represents qualitative content and substance.

Examples of his piano works are seen in his jazz album *Blues and the Abstract Truth* wherein both secular and religious emotions are apparent. Most interesting are *The Meetin'; In Time; Lem and Aide;* and *Shufflin'*, whose beginning measures are shown in Example 52.

Ex. 52. *Shufflin'*, Nelson. © Copyright Edward B. Marks Music Corporation. Used by permission.

Among some of his compositions are: *Hobo Flats; African Sunset; Hoe Down; Miss Fine; Emancipation Blues; Kilimanjar; More Blues; Abstract Truth* (recording); *Blues and the Abstract Truth* (eleven original piano solos); *The Kennedy Dream; Walk on the Wild Side; Who's Afraid of Virginia Woolf?; Ironside* (background score for television show); *Patterns for Saxophone* (textbook on jazz); *Goin' Out of My Head* (w/West Montgomery); *It Takes a Thief* (original background music); and others.

QUINCY JONES (1933-   )

Quincy Jones is a composer, conductor, trumpeter and pianist with some very notable achievements. A native of Chicago, Illinois, he was reared in Bremerton, Washington. He attended Seattle University and later traveled to Boston where he held a scholarship at the Berkeley School of Music. He also traveled to Paris in order to study with Nadia Boulanger and to Rio de Janeiro for study with Villa-Lobos. Many of his musical techniques were also developed as a result of associations with Ray Charles (from whom Jones gleaned many of his feelings for jazz at an early age) and with Clark Terry and others.

Quincy Jones has performed in Europe and America with various ensembles, from groups of his own to those of Dizzy Gillespie and Lionel Hampton. He became vice-president of Mercury Records soon after he returned from a European tour, but he then decided to continue in composition due to a demand for his work. Now the musical director for the

Fig. 21. Quincy Jones.

Bill Cosby Show, Jones has arranged recordings and other hits for many, including Sammy Davis, Count Basie, Billy Eckstine, Sarah Vaughan, Andy Williams, Frank Sinatra, Peggy Lee and others. His film scores have rated Academy Award nominations.

The compositional style of Jones' is an imaginative, astutely interesting mixture of form, unique orchestrations and balance of parts. He employs both an academic approach and a looseness of manner with his materials, and makes use of both tonal and atonal concepts.

Among his works are: *The Four Winds;* Music for the films: *The Pawnbroker; Walk, Don't Run; The Lost Man; In Cold Blood; The Mirage; The Slender Thread; The Boy and the Tree; Sanford and Son;* and *The Bill Cosby Show;* and innumerable recordings: *Walking in Space; Smackwater Jack; Gula Matari and the Black Requiem,* with Ray Charles collaborator.

There are countless other musicians in jazz who are equally representative of the Freedom Era. Donald Byrd, the trumpeter-composer and educator; Cecil Taylor, pianist-composer of avant-garde; Andrew Hill, composer of avant-garde; Ron Carter, string-composer; Archie Shepp, saxophone-composer; Don Cherry, trumpeter-composer; Jaki Byard, pianist-composer; Albert Ayler, Melba Liston, and others.

145

XIV
CONTEMPORARY FORMS, TRENDS AND
COMPOSERS OF THE NEW MUSIC

The forms and styles of the contemporary scene are both traditional and new, and are influenced by both African and western contributions. Art forms range from familiar symphonic forms, chamber music and opera to interludes and hybrids. Popular forms are represented in structures from musicals to rock. Both types experiment with electronic and computer music, filtered to meet the challenges of a tomorrow.

Rock operas, jazz sonatas or symphonies, jazz preludes, jazz masses or blues sonatas are as common as traditional forms and are placed in well organized structures. In addition, forms of electronic and new music in general are composed with titles of tapes, vacuum cleaners, violins or other permutations such as the moog synthesizer.

The primary function of art music is still designed for listening, while jazz and other popular forms have somewhat followed suit, being intended for both active and passive participation. Folk forms and jazz forms are still found mainly in the night clubs, etc., but this music is also performed on concert stages. Rock is still used mainly for dancing and is generally restricted to simple forms and techniques, as are most folk and popular songs.

As forms have changed, so have their concepts. Where composers once established a separation of popular and art music forms through practice of one type, many composers of today openly practice all types and more readily accept all music which they write as art, *per se*. Although many categories of rock, blues and folk are unfortunately written mainly by amateurs who have a lack of either talent or achievement, well-written jazz music, on the other hand, is constantly practiced and promoted by professional and talented musicians. Jazz in particular has now reached the level of art music, and in some cases, is almost indistinguishable from traditional art music forms and techniques.

Compositional Trends

Timbres and orchestrations for all music also show more freedom of choice and change. Partly influenced by jazz instrumentation, guitars, banjos, saxophones and other nontraditional instruments have joined the orchestras for art music, while the flute, violin, oboe and French horn are seen more frequently in jazz. More orchestral instruments also perform in rock, while African instruments also account for many new ideas of timbre.

146

Whereas the latter instruments have performed in popular music before the contemporary era, such practices are becoming more standard than uncommon. Spectacular instrumentation now includes a single player with two or more instruments performing simultaneously, or electric extensions of traditional instruments such as the trumpet, flute, and guitar.

Techniques of contemporary music range from the European major-minor schemes to the African and Asian modal scales. Block chords continue from the modern period of the twentieth century, and polyrhythms and other cross rhythms are standard as well as sporadic and fragmented examples. In addition, dissonances of seconds and sevenths combine with the traditional sounds to present Space Age concepts of music.

Twelve tone music, as practiced by Anton Webern and Arnold Schoenberg, is now a more accustomed sound both in classical music and avant-garde jazz, particularly since the experimental pioneering of electronic sounds. Its lack of emphasis upon a key center promotes the aspect of atonalism and specializes in tone rows, retrogrades, inversions and higher mathematical symbols. This music has also encouraged composers to write music involving extremes in sound and to include half spoken-half sung vocal techniques (Sprechstimme).

Melody, irregularly phrased, may be constructed of three or five measures rather than the traditional two or four. Melodies with irregular meters may also employ a single number placed on the grand staff to denote its triple or duple time.

Many contemporary techniques such as polyrhythm, polymeters and asymmetrical phrases are similar to those discussed in African music. Some aspects of irregular instrumentation, improvisation and asymmetrical form are related, as well as the fusion of scales and chords. Stylistically, atonal music employs many of the African features along with newly contrived methods of composition. While homophonic music does exist today, the new emphasis is mostly on individual polyphonic lines in ensemble and dissonances.

One of the more contemporary concepts of harmony involves the principle of intervallic relationships wherein the distance from one note to another becomes increasingly important. Even though many altered chords result in this process (as harmony results from polyphony) the method of procedure differs from the norm. Within these practices are found tone clusters of close intervals from two to three or more. Its linear style emphasizes the horizontal movement of tones, while the vertical approach places sounds against simultaneous movements. Other features are the displaced tones, or those placed in other registers within the line of melodic tones and chord patterns. These are being used as terminations, beginnings, interpolations or as resolutions of tones or chords from their traditional use. Some of the principal aspects of the new music are seen in Example 53 including symbols of traditional and chance music.

147

Ex. 53. Contemporary symbols and techniques of music.

1. Computer symbols: $\dfrac{I \times I \times I = I}{I \times I \times I}$; $\dfrac{n\,(n-1)}{r}$; $\dfrac{6 \times 5 \times 4 \times 3 \times 2}{3 \times 3 \times 1 \times 1}$

2. Miscellaneous symbols: meters; ties and prolongations; accents and arpeggios.

3. Forms: traditional and new measures.

$2 + 2 = 4$	$2 + 1 = 3$
$4 + 4 = 8$	$3 + 3 = 6$
$8 + 8 = 16$	$3 + 5 = 8$

4. Rhythms.

5. Melodies: asymmetrical; displaced registers.

6. Harmonies: atonal cluster, polytonality, intervals.

7. Scales: pentatonic, twelve tone, diminished; symbols of twelve tone row.

R = Retrograde
I = Inversion
RI = Retrograde Inversion

148

Although definite barriers are outlined in this book in order to classify situations and styles into some organized scheme, it must be stressed that periods and philosophies overlap, making it virtually impossible to place a composer completely within a period or style of writing. This is true particularly in reference to contemporary composers, or in the case of those discussed in the Modern Era who are yet in a state of change. For composers are people who learn and change with each new discovery or innovation. Therefore, modern techniques coincide in part with those of the contemporary era.

The new always retains a part of the old. In this respect, composers already discussed such as Ulysses Kay, Billy Taylor, or Joseph Kennedy could very well be discussed within the contemporary according to some devices in their recent works, and according to their present status in this era.

Composers

The contemporary period is difficult to place as to time or composers. Because periods often overlap in technique and style, and so many diverse practices move in simultaneous procession, no definitive date can be exact. The Modern period of the early 1900's overlaps with the contemporary. However, the 1960's did show more marked differences and freedom in style and ways of composing than did previous years. The period was also a resulting fact of the freedom movement in the present decade. Therefore, this section is devoted to this most recent period.

Contemporary composers are difficult to place or categorize. As to specific practices, today's composers use all available media, styles, emotions and musical types. The tools are no longer the orchestral instruments and voices divided into the elements of music. The structured form may be implied, or may be entirely extemporaneous. It may also be entirely composed note by note. The rhythm may be regular or irregular, strict or obscured. It may even be unsingable. The media may range from car horns to the strings of the piano.

Composers of today are keenly aware of purpose, intent, and character in music. They are also scholars, humanists and seekers of identity. They practice within a freedom of thought never before allowed in the direct merging and acceptance of the merger. Many write third stream music or rock equally as well as they write jazz without the inclusion of art music. The recent trend of jazz being taught in colleges and other institutions has permitted this, as well as the knowledge that jazz has become difficult and "respectable."

Black composers feel the strong need and compulsion for the expression of Self, of a heritage and a national acceptance. By also using the musical tools contributed by a people within this country, both the realization of nationalism and inheritance from another country are fixed. Likewise, the inclusion of blues, spirituals, and jazz as inspirations for compositions further implants nationalism into their music. The direct penetration of African scales and rhythms are some of the most exciting aspects of the music, and are continued in the fusion with European features.

Few composers omit the techniques of twelve tone music, or at least the principles of atonalism. Many are also inspired by electronic devices. Even the noise elements of instruments are part of the equipment for the new music whose sounds reflect immediate substances of the present, of life, reality and change.

GEORGE THEOPHILUS WALKER (1922-   )

George Walker, a composer-pianist of repute, was born in Washington, D.C., and currently lives in Northampton, Massachusetts. He was educated at Oberlin College (Mus. B.); Curtis Institute of Music in Philadelphia (Artist Diploma); American Academy in Fontainebleau, France; the Eastman School of Music in Rochester, New York (Artist Diploma and Doctorate); and has further studied in Paris with Nadia Boulanger in composition and with Curzon and Casadesus in piano at Fontainebleau. He has also studied with Rudolf Serkin, Rosario Scalero, Piatigorsky, Primrose, and Menotti.

Walker has taught extensively in various capacities. He has served at the Curtis Institute of Music as an assistant to Rudolf Serkin, and has taught at Dillard University in New Orleans, at the Dalcroze School of Music in New York, at Smith College, the New School of Social Research, and at Rutgers University.

For his work as pianist and composer, his honors have included scholarships and fellowships from Oberlin, Eastman, John Hay Whitney, The MacDowell, the Bennington Composers Conference, the American Symphony League and the American Music Center, as well as the Guggenheim and Rockefeller Foundations. In 1945, Walker was a winner of the Philadelphia Youth Auditions where he appeared as soloist with the Philadelphia Orchestra with Eugene Ormandy as conductor. In 1945, he was awarded a Town Hall debut by Efrem Zimbalist. In 1958, he was again awarded a Town Hall recital by Mrs. Efrem Zimbalist.

As a concert pianist, he has made numerous tours of the United States, Europe, Canada, and the West Indies. The Bok Award for concerts in Europe as a piano soloist was awarded in 1963. As a composer, he has merited an equal number of honors. The Rhea Sosland Chamber Music Contest brought him an award for his *String Quartet* in 1967; the Harvey Gaul Prize for the *Sonata for Two Pianos* in 1964; and a citation from Eastman for contributions to the field of music.

He composes for voices, orchestral instruments, piano, and various combinations. Highly difficult, complex and technically demanding, his music is both tonal and atonal and deals with contemporary idioms in sound and form. Linear independency is shown in lyrical idioms. Orchestrations of sound may occur in blended homophony or percussive blocks of atonal notes. Irregular intervals and extremities of complex rhythms and registers mark his style of composition.

150

Fig. 22. George Walker.

Fig. 23. Hale Smith.

Among his works are: *So We'll Go A-roving; The Bereaved Maid; Lament; I Went to Heaven; Gloria in Memoriam* (for women's voices); *Two Poems; Piano Sonatas Nos. 1 & 2; Sonata for Violin and Piano; Stars* for mixed chorus; *Sonata for Cello and Piano; Spatials* (for piano); *Fifteen Songs; Concerto for Trombone and Orchestra; String Quartet; Ten Works for Chorus; Perimeters for Clarinet and Piano; Three Lyrics* for chorus; and others.

HALE SMITH (1925-   )

Hale Smith was born in Cleveland, Ohio, and has now become a resident of Freeport, Long Island, New York. An energetic free-lance composer, arranger, lecturer and performer, Smith was educated at the Cleveland Institute of Music where he studied with Ward Lewis and received the B.M. and M.M. degrees. He also studied composition with Marcel Dick and others. Smith has lectured extensively; he is associate professor at the University of Connecticut; he is an Adjunct Associate Professor of music at the Post College of Long Island University and is editor of Sam Fox Co.

A solid and confident composer whose works command a proper respect and attention for their sound content and their technical applications, he has been hailed by the late Arthur Loesser and Herbert Elwell as a "huge, rich and significant talent." For his work, honors and awards have earned him frequent public performances, citations and commissions. His *Contours for Orchestra* was commissioned by Broadcast Music, Inc., as part of its twentieth anniversary celebrations. He was a winner of the Broadcast Music Student Composers Award in 1953. His works have been performed by the Society of Black Composers, the Louisville Orchestra, the Cleveland Orchestra, the Symphony of the New World, the Cincinnati Orchestra, pianist Ward Davenny, the Tougaloo College Choir and others.

A composer in virtually all types of modern music, Smith has composed third stream music, popular and art music, and has engaged in projects from publishing to arranging and performing. In the field of jazz, Smith has arranged for Chico Hamilton, Oliver Nelson, Quincy Jones, Eric Dolphy, Ahmad Jamal, and others. His original compositions have included music for television dramas, documentary films, recordings and for numerous dramatic and concert occasions. He is also active in various organizations. In the American Composers Alliance, he serves on the Board of Governors and has recently been elected to the Board of Directors of Composers Recordings, Inc.

Smith composes chamber music as well as solo and ensemble vocal music. Although his music is contemporary, his techniques range from traditional chords to the most difficult twelve tone varieties, altered chords, clusters and polyphony. His music possesses dynamic sounds and shows improvisatory characteristics, cadenzas of virtuosic flare, trills and other compositional techniques.

Melodically, Smith employs repetitions of tones. In such cases, both

152

the rhythm and harmony become main factors of interest. He also uses traditional skips of thirds, diatonic tones, octaves and fifths in exclusive skill. Always tastefully and logically written, his works show both a vocal and instrumental sensitivity.

His rhythms are both complex and simple. However, even when seemingly simple, many are ingenious and challenging. Meters are clear in the use of either common time or more complex ones. Some of the cadences use long rhythmic terminations, while others end on short notes; the general movement of rhythms are fairly uniform.

Harmonically, all techniques of homophony and polyphony are employed in the music. Certain examples of his music are also conceived from the intervallic approach, as in *Three Brevities* for solo flute. His *Faces of Jazz* for piano shows an uncluttered style of merging jazz harmonies and classical techniques. Partly based on blues, fugues, and tin pan, the piece uses consonances, dissonances, ostinato basses, lyricism, and complex rhythms to support the body of emotions and techniques therein. His *Evocation* for piano and the *In Memoriam — Beryl Rubinstein* for chorus show still another style from simple homophony to improvisation. Other works show blocks of sound, full harmonies and an advanced style of writing for all media.

The Three Brevities for solo flute is an unaccompanied example employing the dodecaphonic trends and atonal features of contemporary music. Written in three movements, it outlines exciting melodic and rhythmic characteristics:

Ex. 54. *Three Brevities*, Smith. © Copyright Edward B. Marks Music Corporation. Used by permission.

The *Music for Harp and Orchestra* outlines a most complex organization of rhythms and harmonies. Swiftly passing chords indicated by full orchestral sounds in blocks, clusters, and various intervals are placed against long melodic lines of atonal quality. A portion of the work is illustrated in Example 55 and is scored for violins 1 and 2, violas, celli, basses, alto flute, piccolo, oboe, clarinet, horns, bassoons and harp.

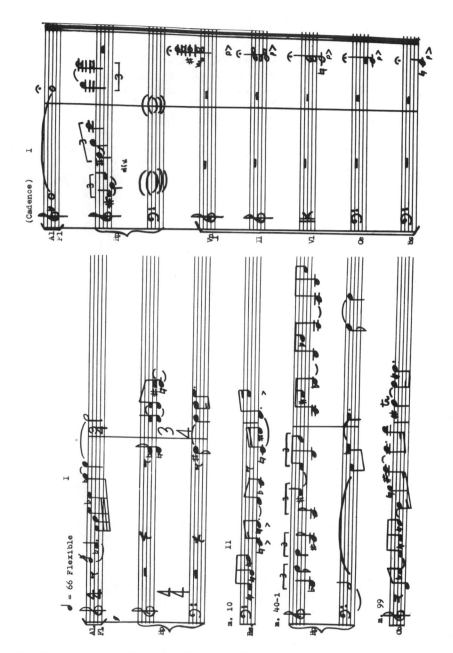

Ex. 55. *Music for Harp and Orchestra*, Smith. © Copyright Edward B. Marks Music Corporation. Used by permission.

Among Hale Smith's works are: scores for Lorca's *Yerma* and *Blood Wedding; In Memoriam — Beryl Rubinstein* (chorus); *Epicedial Variations; Sonata for Cello and Piano; Two Love Songs of John Donne* (soprano and nine instruments); *Three Brevities for Flute; Contours for Orchestra;* score for *Bold New Approach; Somersault* (band); *Take A Chance* (band); *Evocation* (piano); *Orchestral Set; Music for Harp and Orchestra; Three Songs for Voice; Trinial Dance* (elementary band); *By Yearning and by Beautiful* (string orchestra); *Faces of Jazz* (piano pieces); *Comes Tomorrow* (jazz cantata); and others.

ARTHUR CUNNINGHAM (1928-   )

Arthur Cunningham, composer, author, conductor, pianist and bass player was born in Nyack, New York, where he now resides. Educated at the Metropolitan Music School, Fisk University, the Juilliard School of Music and Columbia Teachers College, he has studied with John Work, Peter Menin, Norman Lloyd, Henry Brandt, Peter Wilhousky, Margaret Hillis, and others. A precocious beginner at the age of six, Cunningham began with piano. He wrote and performed piano pieces at the age of seven and eventually graduated to various other instruments at a later time.

Brilliantly alive in both philosophy and professionalism, Cunningham is a firm believer in special aims and standards for the serious music student. He describes his attitudes as representing "a new departure in professional education in the field of music, and addresses itself to those who seek a more thorough training . . . . a high degree of excellence and a sophistication of artistic expression designed to contribute to the profession and to the country as a whole." In realistic terms, his music has shown that his talent can indeed be used to encourage the production of a new breed of musical participants in whom sound training in technique and style can be instilled. Cunningham sums up the educational curriculum as one which must stress the aspects of music as well as related businesses or commercialism. He feels, "To know music is not enough, one must also know life". As a member of ASCAP and ACA, Cunningham writes various source materials and articles and gives lectures and seminars about music.

Cunningham is rich in both experience and awards. In Special Services, he wrote for the army band and toured with a trio as a string bass player. As a student at the Metropolitan Music School, he appeared frequently on radio station WNYC in the performance of his works. He has played double bass with the Suburban Symphony, Rockland County, and has served with the Rockland County Summer Theater as musical director. He has written *Ostrich Feathers* and *Violetta* for the stage. In addition, he has written innumerable compositions for piano, chorus, solo voices, orchestra and various other instrumental combinations. He has written ballets, opera, string quartets, chamber music, and approximately 400 popular songs, as well as ballads, rock and jazz compositions. Among his advanced works for shows, revues, television and art music concerts are works for such musicals as *Patsy Parch, Susan's Dream* and *Ostrich*

155

Fig. 24. Arthur Cunningham.

Feathers, (a rock musical) and *His Natural Grace* (a one-act mini-rock opera).

His honors and awards are seen in performances of his works, commissions and grants. His own works have been performed on programs with those of Howard Swanson. His commissions have come from Fisk University, the Suburban Symphony, the Rockland County Composers and the New World Symphony, as well as Earle Madison. The *Eclatette for Cello* was requested for the 1970 Tschaikowsky Competition in Moscow, Russia; the *Ostrich Feathers* was premiered at the Martinique Theatre, New York City, in 1964; *Concentrics* was premiered at Philharmonic Hall in 1969 (by the New World Symphony); and his works have enjoyed many other performances.

Cunningham considers virtually every style of writing and every form, both sacred and secular. His music is freedom expressed in sound, thinly veiled with a demand that offers no freedom of relaxation in spirit or performance. His music employs a meticulous care as to directions for dynamics, control, rhythms, and techniques. With dynamics sometimes appearing on each phrase of two to three or more notes, they sometimes appear in each measure. The use of grace notes, slides, trills and various meters are also typical of his music. He, like Baker, is apt to use closely aligned meters of 5/4, 2/4, 4/4, 9/8, 5/8, or 3/4. In addition, he uses no meters at all whenever there is a desire for complete freedom of movement.

Both diatonic and irregular melodies are typical. Always melodic, despite his rhythmic interest, each musical element seems equally important to the overall effect. Short and long phrases are frequently arranged against repetitions of a beginning or ending of a melody, augmented or diminished around the fragments of the original. The fragments, in turn, are used to "break" the linear or harmonic motions, or are interpolated as the main melody shifts registers. These fragments also introduce and conclude phrases or sections.

Cunningham has written in both tonal and atonal forms, making use of both traditional western scales and of modal and serial techniques. One example of his work, *Thisby,* a lament for flute and cello (or by cello alone) was adapted from the characters Thisby and Pyramus from his own *A Mid-Summer Nights Dream.* Composed in 1968, it moves in linear patterns interspersed with arpeggi from the cello line. The opening measures of the first movement show no meter:

Ex. 56. *Lament from Thisby,* Cunningham. Used by permission of the composer-publisher.

After the brief introduction, the cello begins in fifths in accompaniment to the chromatic melody of the flute:

Ex. 57.

The flute, in the middle of the composition (section A or "Essay"), again makes use of the barless measures with attractive trills, grace notes and sixteenths:

Ex. 58.

Although the entire piece emphasizes the atonal, the beginning and the ending of the piece outline the C major triad. A unique element of the ending is the indefinite pitch markings in the slurred, downward slide effect common to jazz:

Ex. 59. Excerpts from *Thisby,* Cunningham. Used by permission of composer-publisher.

Some of Cunningham's finest compositional and pianistic techniques occur in a piece for piano, *Engrams,* an atonal structure whose multi-sections vary between slow and fast portions of different thematic materials and moods, indicated in Example 60.

Ex. 60. *Engrams,* Cunningham. Used by permission of composer-publisher.

Among Cunningham's other works are the following: *Two Haitian Play Dances; Four Shadows* (piano); *Sugarhill* (piano); *Engrams* (60 piano pieces); *Amen; Hymn of Our Lord; In the Year Seventeen* (choral); *Ring Out Wild Bells* (choral); *Fruitful Trees More Fruitful Are* (choral); *Organ Prelude and Hymn* (choral); *When I Was One and Twenty* (choral); *He Met Her at the Dolphin* (choral); *Fifty Stars* (female voices); *Into My Heart* (female); *From Where I Stand* (choral); *The Gingerbread Man* (male); *Then The Cricket Sings* (choral); *Song of Songs* (soprano); *Turning of the Babies in the Bed* (baritone); *Jabberwocky* (soprano); *Midsummer Nights Dream* (soprano with instruments); *Forty Pieces* (jazz orchestra); *Adagio for Oboe and Strings; Jazz Pieces* (band); *Ballet* (string quartet, jazz); *Concentrics* (orchestra); *Dim Du Mim* (English horn, orchestra); *Lullabye for a Jazz Baby* (orchestra); *Eclatette for Cello; Dialogue for Piano and Chamber Orchestra; Perimeters for Flute,* clarinet, vibraharp, and double bass); *Louey Louey* (mini-rock opera); *Violette; Ostrich Feathers; Trio for Flute, Viola and Bassoon;* and many others.

THOMAS J. ANDERSON (1928-   )

Thomas J. Anderson, composer-in-residence with the Atlanta Symphony Orchestra for the 1969-70 season, and now a composer at Tufts University in Massachusetts, was born in Coatesville, Pennsylvania. Educated at West Virginia State College, Pennsylvania State University, the Cincinnati Conservatory and the State University of Iowa, he has also taught at West Virginia State, Langston University, Prairie View and Tennessee A&I University.

A member of ACA, he has held fellowships at the MacDowell Colony in Peterborough, New Hampshire, from 1960-68 and was given commissions by the Oklahoma City Junior Symphony Orchestra, and West Virginia State College. He won the Fromm Foundation Award in 1964, and the Copley Foundation Award in 1964.

159

Anderson has described his own style as one whose "works show the adaptations of pluralistic values which range reflects the influence of primitive music jazz, post-Webern, and avant-garde styles. I feel that it is the duty of the composer to make audible the inaudible and thus link some part of mankind. The compositions do not represent any style or school of composition but seek a continuous arrangement of sound in a given time and place context. Its only meaning grows out of my experience with humanity and therefore manifests a genetic state of flux."

Anderson also describes the style and tendencies of compositional technique in the following manner: "The projection and receding of instrumental colors at different levels of densities tend to produce sound platforms within dynamic possibilities. The works are organized around motific sets or small patterns of notes which function in many types of musical environment associations. Emphasis is on the use of effects which relate directly to the musical ideas. Melodies tend to be predominantly disjunct and show a preference for symmetrical rhythm. These ideas are expanded by use of numerical proportionalism, multirhythmic values and metric modulation. Compositions, in general, favor a plastic single movement structure in which there exist a series of cause and effect relationships. The mood within sections tends to run a wide gamut of densities, ranges of sound elements, developmental manipulations, and the free distribution of independent units. Harmony functions from a linear context and tends to be identified with free atonalism."

In many cases, the titles do not reveal the forms of his pieces, giving a semi-unorthodox air to his art. For example, *Six Etudes and a Fancy* is a piece for woodwind quintet and *Squares* is an essay or orchestral piece. These terms are used rather than "symphony" or "woodwind quintet". On the other hand, Anderson appears, in some respects, within the art music tradition rather than of third stream or jazz. In no way, however, does this make him a conservative composer, for his style is influenced by many of the same elements and techniques of which jazz is composed, and his works are undoubtedly contemporary.

Melodically, Anderson is sensitive to the medium at hand and the emotion desired. He uses both diatonic and wide skips, within short fragmentary phrases or an extraordinarily long one. He may also write two lines in intervals of the second or other dissonances, interspersing the lines with major or minor resolutions. His free choice of materials of composition are not restrictive in his stress on either chromaticism or diatonicism, tonality on atonality.

Rhythmically, sixteenth notes move to dotted eighths in schematic successions or from fast to very slow (such as from an eighth or sixteenth to a tied whole note). At times, there are rows of eighths in succession being interrupted by a rest, dot or tie to effect syncopation. Meters and polymeters from 4/2 to 12/8 and 4/4 are used distinctly with dynamic extremes. One meter sign found in *Chamber Symphony* simply shows the symbol of "four" being placed above a quarter note: (𝟒). Other rhythmic notations are seen in Example 61.

Ex. 61. Rhythms of Anderson.

Harmonically, Anderson uses homophony, but appears more linear in style as he emphasizes the instrumental independencies of each instrument, giving special and individual attention to the typical needs and extensions of all. Low and high register instruments are written to explore the realms of possibilities.

An example of some demands required by the chorus part of *Personals,* in addition to singing, are such dramatics as spoken lines in discordant fashion shaped into the score above the narrator and orchestral part at measures 177-81, Example 62.

Ex. 62. *Personals,* Anderson. © 1967, T. J. Anderson, Jr. All rights reserved including the right of public performance for profit. Reprinted by permission of American Composers Alliance.

161

Sometimes the melodic and harmonic aspects become inseparable in either a polyphonic setting or in an interchange of one melody being extended from voice part to voice part, as in measures 183-187 of the same composition:

Ex. 63. *Personals,* Anderson. © 1967, T. J. Anderson, Jr. All rights reserved including the right of public performance for profit. Reprinted by permission of American Composers Alliance.

Whenever Anderson uses homophony, the fullness of sounds as reflected in the cadential progression of the harpsichord part of his *Five Bagatelles* is typical of the possibilities. Composed for oboe, violin and harpsichord, the piece contains five movements based on dance rhythms and folk forms such as the fourth movement, entitled *Blues.* Excerpted below, the piece uses no key signature and stresses no tonal center, as its characteristic dissonances are set at its opening by minor seconds. Another composition, *Five Portraitures* for two pianos, exhibits a barless movement, entitled *Contemplation,* which has difficult rhythms and atonal harmonies (Examples 64 and 65).

162

He has written piano duos and solos, chamber ensembles, chorus and orchestral pieces, many of which have been widely performed. His most important works are *Five Portraitures of Two People* for piano duo; *Squares* for orchestra; *Connections,* a fantasy for string quintet; *Rotations* for band; *Chamber Symphony; New Dances* for orchestra; *Classical Symphony; Six Pieces for Clarinet* and *Chamber Orchestra; Five Bagatelles for Oboe, Violin, and Harpsichord; Symphony in Three Movements; Five Etudes and a Fancy* for woodwind quintet; *Personals,* a cantata; *Rotations* for band; *In Memoriam Zack Walker;* and many others.

163

NOEL G. DA COSTA (1930-   )

Noel Da Costa, composer-violinist, was born in Lagos, Nigeria. He was taken to the West Indies at three years of age and later to America at the age of eleven. Da Costa now resides in New York City and works as a free-lance violinist while composing, recording, concertizing and teaching at Rutgers University. Currently a violinist in the accompanying orchestra for *Promises, Promises,* Da Costa was educated at Queens College and Columbia University. He has also been the deserving recipient of a Fulbright Scholarship to Italy where he studied with Dallapiccolo during the 1958-60 season.

A member of the Black Society of Composers, he has taught at Hampton Institute, Hunter College and Queens College. In addition, part of his time has involved concerts at Colleges and other institutions in and around New York and in the South.

His *Five Verses with Vamps* was performed by Ronald Lipscomb, cellist, and Charles Burkhart, pianist, at the Queens College Concert in 1969. Although most of his works have been composed for art music ensembles and soloists, he has recently been commissioned to write semi-jazz and rock pieces which have also been performed.

Da Costa's music moves toward all the possibilities of harmonic, melodic and rhythmic features of the contemporary era. However, definite linear qualities predominate, with intervallic tendencies planned where chords might otherwise be. Dramatic leaps compete with diatonic and chromatic devices, and twelve tone rows and their retrogrades dot the pages in daring parallels, contrary motions, discordant agreement, improvisations and other interpolations resembling architecture. Highly critical and conscientious in his projects, he proceeds scholarly toward each composition as though it were the study of life itself.

Among his works are: *Five Verses with Vamps* for cello and piano; *The Confession Stone* for soprano and ten instruments; *Extempore Blue; The Singing Tortoise* (a play for children scored for soprano, baritone, narrator and chorus, and accompanied by flute, percussion, temple blocks and bongos); and *Cikan Cimalo* for electric guitars, fender bass and percussion; *Silver-Blue* (flute); *Three Short Pieces* and others.

FREDERICK C. TILLIS (1930-   )

Frederick C. Tillis, composer-performer, arranger and conductor, was born in Galveston, Texas. Having taught in Frankfort, Kentucky, where he was head of the Department of Music and professor of composition, he now serves at the University of Massachusetts. Having been educated at Wiley College and the University of Iowa, where he received the M.A. and Ph.D. degrees in composition, Tillis is a talented composer of technical strength and praiseworthy ingenuity. Widely performed and well received, his music should soon become standard repertoire in western music.

Tillis was appointed director of the 3560th Air Force Band in 1954, for which he wrote and arranged music. He has served as a teacher at Wiley College and Grambling College, and has often been invited to participate in forums and lectures as well as to conduct various ensembles. Upon such occasions, he served as guest composer at the 1967 Symposium of Contemporary Music at Illinois Wesleyan University, where his chamber works were performed, and also the Festival of Contemporary music at Spelman College in 1968, where his *Design for Orchestra No. 2* was performed by the Atlanta Symphony Orchestra with Robert Shaw as conductor.

Tillis utilizes various source materials for content. Twelve tone composition, free composition, frequently with lyrical pantonal melodies and terse harmonic textures, as well as features from periods other than contemporary. In addition, jazz rhythms typify certain of his movements. He explores most effectively the extreme ends of instrumental resources. In addition to scoring for band, orchestra, chorus, solo voices, and chamber ensembles, he also makes use of non-conventional methods of using instruments such as the "fixed" strings of the piano (a la Cage).

Mixtures of major, minor and other chromatic and diatonic practices are employed on both traditional and non-traditional forms. In addition to regular chordal and scalewise procedures, leaps, octaves, pluckings, slaps or drumming effects, impressionistic extensions of sound and dissonances characterize his music. From the guitar-effect of the piano to the aesthetic beauty of a major chord being plucked in approximate tones against the reverberation of a glissando in motion, the unpredictable, but interesting style of Tillis resounds.

Among his compositions are: *Passacaglia for Brass Quintet; Quartet for Flute, Clarinet, Bassoon and Cello; The End of All Flesh, baritone and piano; A Prayer in Faith; Psalms, baritone and piano; Capriccio for Viola and Piano; Concert Piece for Clarinet and Piano; Overture to a Dance, band; Militant Mood for Brass Sextet; String Trio; Phantasy for Viola and Piano; Passacaglia for Organ in Baroque Style; Brass Quintet; Quintet for Four Woodwinds and Percussion; Three Movements for Piano; Motions for Trombone and Piano; Music for Alto Flute, Cello and Piano; Sequences and Burlesque, for strings; Two Songs for Soprano and Piano; Music for an Experimental Lab, Ensemble No. 1; Gloria: Music for An Experimental Lab, Ensemble No. 2; Freedom — Memorial for Dr. Martin Luther King, Jr., for chorus; Music for Tape Recorder No. 1; Three Plus One, for Guitar, clarinet and tape; Alleluia for chorus;* and others.

DAVID BAKER (1931-   )

David Baker, composer, conductor, author, educator and cellist, was born in Indianapolis, Indiana. He presently resides in Indiana where he teaches at Indiana University and heads the Jazz Department. He was educated at Indiana University where he received the Bachelor's and Master's degrees in music education. He has also studied with several musicians such as John Lewis, J. J. Johnson, Gunther Schuller, Murray Grodner, George Russell, Russell Brown, Thomas Beversdorf and others.

Baker has taught at Lincoln University in Missouri, the Indianapolis Public Schools and Indiana Central College. In addition, his professional

165

experiences have included numerous tours, concerts, lectures and workshops in various countries. He has traveled extensively with Quincy Jones, and has played with other jazz groups such as Stan Kenton, Maynard Ferguson, Lionel Hampton, and the Wes Montgomery Sextet. His performances have not been restricted to jazz, for Baker has also performed with the Indiana University Philharmonic; the Indiana University Opera Orchestra; the Indiana University Wind and Brass Ensembles; the Butler University Orchestra, Band and Brass Ensembles; and the Indiana Central College String Quartet.

A musical giant of great talent, Baker is competent on several instruments: piano, tuba, trombone, and bass. He has performed as soloist with the Boston Symphony and the Evansville Philharmonic. As conductor, he was invited to lead the Indianapolis Symphony & Civic Orchestras, and the Indiana University Concert Symphony Orchestra. In addition, his own groups of octet, quintet, or "ensembles" have performed extensively in concerts and on recordings.

Honors for Baker have come from the Indianapolis Jazz Club, Inc., which made him a lifetime member. He holds membership in Gamma Tau Chapter of Phi Mu Alpha Sinfonia, the Indiana Philharmonic Gold Award, and from Lenox School of Jazz and Indiana University. He has also been awarded the *Downbeat* New Star Award, and the Outstanding Musician Award from the National Association of Negro Musicians.

Baker's works, over 100 in number, consist of mass media types from religious to secular themes, third stream music, art music, and jazz. His works also range from orchestral ensembles to piano solos and other combinations. Baker has also authored source books on jazz improvisation and contemporary music.

His style of writing, based upon time and change in the Space Age, elect versatility and order, measured against improvisation and plan. Polymeters, tempo markings of "fast", "slow", "nonchalant", "medium blues", or "lazily", along with traditional European markings are used.

Though rhythmically interesting, Baker uses melody well. The *Cello Sonata,* for example, begins with a beautiful theme which moves in triplets toward polymetric values of meticulous intricacy. He makes use of altered tonic chords and of ninths, elevenths as well as atonalism. The opening bars of the *Sonata* are excerpted:

Ex. 66. *Sonata for Cello and Piano,* Baker. Used by permission of the composer.

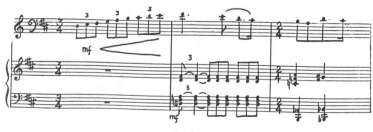

166

Fig. 25. David Baker.

In addition to the sequences, parallelism, polytonality, polymeters, and double stops, there are lyrical melodies and large intervallic jumps and altered tones for the cellist, with challenging technical problems. The overall harmonies are traditional, as well as atonal. Some chords are composed in fourths and clusters rather than in the customary thirds. The termination of the piece consists of a D major chord, while the piano support uses polychordal features, thereby distorting the emphasis of the D major texture, as seen in the last cadence of the first movement:

Ex. 67.

167

Another composition, a *Piano Sonata* dedicated to Natalie Hinderas, concert pianist, is composed of three movements entitled *Black Art, A Song After Paul Lawrence Dunbar,* and *Coltrane* (reference to jazz musician). The traditional form of the sonata becomes real to the trained listener in that the first movement follows the conventional "sonata-allegro" form while the titles captivate and invite attention with elements of blues, jazz and classicism. The use of octaves, chromatics, glissandos, imitation, and the outer extremities of the keyboard together with dynamic contrasts are used in challenging concensus of atonalism, polymeters and cross rhythms. The opening bars and measures 19-20 of the first movement are shown in Example 68.

Ex. 68. *Piano Sonata,* Baker. Used by permission of the composer.

The second movement is based on the same material as *A Song,* from his cycle of *Five Songs for Soprano and Piano.* Inspired by the Black poetry of Paul Lawrence Dunbar, the vocal melody is simulated in the right hand of the piano version in an ultra-lyrical style. Both versions are shown in Example 69.

Ex. 69. *A Song* (vocal art song), Baker. Used by permission of the composer.

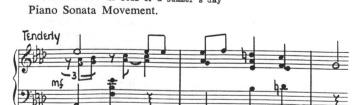

Piano Sonata Movement.

Among the numerous works of Baker are the following: *Dream Boogie*, for chorus; *Black America — to the Memory of Martin Luther King Jr.*; *Black Thursday* (jazz ensemble); *But I am a Worm* (mixed voices); *Catalyst* (*jazz ensemble*); *Deliver My Soul* (*voices, dancers and jazz ensemble*); *A dollar Short and a Day Late* (*jazz ensemble*); *The Dude* (*cello and piano*); *Hymn and Deviation* (*brass, quartet*); *I Am Poured Out Like Water* (*male voices and strings*); *Jazz Mass* (*voices and jazz septer*); *Catholic Mass for Peace* (*chorus and jazz ensemble*); *Le Chat Qui Peche* (*jazz ensemble*); *Concerto* (*violin and jazz ensemble*); *John Coltrane in Memoriam* (*jazz ensemble*); *Lutheran Mass* (*Introit soprano and piano*); *Masque of the Read Death* (*ballet*), (*unfinished*); *Passion* (*jazz ensemble*); *Quartet No. 1* (*strings*); *Sonata* (*violin and piano*); *Sonata* (*cello and piano*); *Splooch* (*jazz ensemble*); *That's the Way, Lord Nelson* (*trumpet, saxophone and double bass*); *Verism* (*jazz ensemble*); *Thou Doest Lay Me in the Dust of Death* (*voices and strings*); *Abyss* (*soprano and piano*); *Afro-Cuban Suite* (*band*); *The Screamin' Meemies* (*jazz ensemble*); *Le Roi* (*jazz ensemble*); *Soul on Ice* (*jazz ensemble*); *Al-ki-hol* (*jazz ensemble*); *All the Ends of the Earth Shall Remember* (*mixed voices and string orchestra*); *Ballads* (*saxophone, horn and violin and cello*); *Beatitudes* (*chorus, narrator, dances and orchestra*); *Romanza and March* (*three trombones*); many others. Baker has also written publications of *Jazz Improvisation; Developing Improvisational Technique, based on the Lydian Concept; Developing Improvisational Facility with II-V Progression; Developing Improvisational Facility with the Turnback* and others are in progress.

COLERIDGE-TAYLOR PERKINSON (1932-   )

Coleridge-Taylor Perkinson, composer, conductor and educator, was born in New York. He was educated at New York University and the Manhattan School of Music (where he received the Bachelor and Master of Music degrees). He also did further work at the Berkshire Music Center in choral conducting, and in orchestral conducting at the Mozarteum, the Netherlands Radio Union and the Hilversum. His wide experience in compositional studies has included Vittorio Gianninni, Charles Mills and Earl Kim as his teachers.

As an educator, Perkinson has served as music director of the Professional Children's School and as a faculty member of Manhattan School of Music and Brooklyn College. He has also held the positions of assistant conductor of the Dessoff Choirs and conductor of the Brooklyn Community Symphony Orchestra.

As evidenced by the various titles and commissions which he has received from the Arthur Mitchell Dance Company, the Lou Rawls Special, the Barbara McNair Television Show, the Martin Luther King Film Production, the Jayjen Productions and U.S.I.A., Perkinson has undertaken many challenges in composition. His skill has also been exhibited on recordings with Donald Byrd, Max Roach and others. Of his most out-

Fig. 26. Coleridge-Taylor Perkinson.

standing works are those for ballet, chorus and orchestral ensembles, films, theatre, vocal and piano music.

His style ranges from the conventional to the unconventional, with both tonal and atonal examples of writing being portrayed to fair advantage. A typical feature is to use extremities of sound or of widely placed accompaniments against closely woven voices. Also characteristic are blocks of sound (as in various representations within the *Fredome-Freedom* work for chorus and piano), polymeters and sectionalism. Perkinson also uses approximations of pitches, glissandos, syncopations and other technically difficult idioms of tonal and polytonal varieties.

Among his compositions are: *String Quartet* No. 1 — *Calvary; Variations and Fugue* on *The Ash Grove* for violin and piano; *Sonatina for Percussion; Piano Sonata; Psalm Twenty Three; Fredome-Freedom; Songs to Spring; Thirteen Love Songs in Jazz Settings; Concerto for Viola and Orchestra; Grass Poem* for piano, strings and percussion; *Ode to Otis; Man Better Man* (w/Erroll Hill); and others.

170

CARMAN MOORE (1936-   )

Carman Moore, a composer, author and performer, is currently a teacher at his own private studio in New York City. He also lectures at Manhattan College, Yale University and other institutions, writes articles on music subjects for the *Village Voice* newspaper and serves as president of the Society of Black Composers. Once a student at Oberlin Conservatory, Moore graduated from Ohio State University and attended the Juilliard School of Music where he earned the Master's degree. He was a student of Hall Overton, Vincent Persichetti and Luciano Berio.

Moore, whose works were represented in Washington during the International Festival of Contemporary Music in 1968, is an award-winning composer of chamber music, theatrical and vocal works. Commissions have come from the New York City Ballet, the Anna Sokolow Dance Company and from other festivals and institutions who recognize his musical talents.

JOHN CARTER (1937-   )

John Carter, a talented pianist-composer, was born in St. Louis, Missouri. Traveling to New York where he established significant advancements in his writing and performance opportunities, he later moved to Washington in 1968, upon acceptance of the honor of composer-in-residence with the Washington National Symphony Orchestra. He received his education at Oberlin University, and received grants from the Rockefeller Foundation, the American Music Center and the ASCAP organization.

Once a teacher of the new Federal City College in Washington, D.C., Carter became recognized as an early entrant into the mainstream of American composers when his works were performed by concert artists such as Betty Allen, Martina Arroyo, Leontyne Price, George Shirley, Adele Addison, William Warfield and Julius Katchen. In addition to the *Requiem Seditiosam* which both he and Katchen have performed, his orchestral version has enjoyed a performance by the Washington Symphony with Howard Mitchell as conductor. The same piece had already received its premiere at the Philharmonic Hall at the Lincoln Center in New York City. In 1967, an entire program devoted to Carter's works was given at the New York Public Library-Museum of Performing Arts at Lincoln Center, which included his *Cantata,* a published work. The reviews were favorable.

The New York Times' Raymond Ericson wrote of his *Saetas Profanas* as being as "fine as anything . . . an effective vocalise." Of the same work, the Hagerstown, Virginia, *Evening News* and the Delta County *Independent* of Colorado termed it "A tremendous offering" and as having "excited everyone." Other reviews have found his works "impelling," "breathtaking *tours de force,*" "beautiful, delicate and dramatic," and "Sensitive lyricism and deeply poetic." Carter has also received complimentary reviews of his own piano playing. As a pianist he has won competitions in many cities throughout the United States.

171

Fig. 27. John Carter.

Composed of both traditional and contemporary elements, his compositions have been written with an emphasis upon melodic and harmonic imitation, thematic interchange and motive relationships which bridge polytonalities and tonal structures rather than atonal examples effected by the times. At intervals, his full chords, chromatics, extended intervals, clustered tones, dissonances and consonances together obscure the major or minor feeling only temporarily. Chords built in fourths, fifths, and other unusual combinations prevail in alternation with the traditional. Melodic, rhythmic and harmonic repetitions are used as effective descriptions of the subject.

His sensitivity in writing provides a just presentation of the instruments in his list of works, a freshness of style and a beckoning of the lively aspects at his disposal. Both emotional and serious in content, Carter has borrowed from the blues (especially for the *Valses*), the spirituals and from the era in which he lives in order to mold his compositions.

His *Cantata* for voice and piano shows his style of simplicity of ideas with a complex foundation of techniques discussed above. Containing five parts or movements, it consists of a prelude, rondo, recitative, air and toccata, and shows a developing style mixed with either no meter at all, or with polymeters ranging from 8/8 to 5/4. Carefully marked with dynamic extremes and directions for performance, the piece makes use of barless measures, improvisational effects producing a flow of interesting rhythms from the simple to the complex. The work, excerpted in Example 70, gives a feeling of direction and character:

Ex. 70   Prelude and Rondo Openings, from *Cantata*, Carter. © 1964, Southern Music Publishing Co., Inc. Used by permission.

Carter has written the following works: *Cantata; Epigrams* (ballet); *Requiem Seditiosam; In Memoriam, Medgar Evers* for orchestra; *Valses Pour Les Danseurs Noirs* (Waltzes for Black Dancers and piano); *Saetas Profanas; Japanese Poems; Emblemes* for violin; *Piano Concerto* and others.

173

Olly Wilson, composer, bass-violist, was born in St. Louis, Missouri. He attended Washington University in St. Louis, received the Master of Music degree from the University of Illinois and the doctorate from the University of Iowa. As a pupil of Robert Wykes, Robert Kelley and Phillip Bezanson, he studied composition and electronic work at the Studio for Experimental Music at the University of Illinois.

Wilson has performed on the bass with several orchestras, including the St. Louis Philharmonic Orchestra, the St. Louis Summer Players and the Cedar Rapids Symphony Orchestra. As a teacher, he has instructed at Florida A & M University, West Virginia University and the University of California at Berkeley. A recipient of the 1968 Dartmouth Arts Council Prize, he was also awarded the prize at the first International Competition for Electronic Compositions for his work *Cetus*. At present, Wilson is studying African music on a Guggenheim grant.

Orchestras such as the Dallas Symphony Orchestra, the Minneapolis Symphony Orchestra and the Atlanta Symphony have performed his works. A composer of chamber works, vocal works, orchestral and electronic works, his compositions have also received numerous hearings. Some of his pieces were rendered at the Music Educators' National Conference Black Music Workshop in Chicago in 1970, and at the 1967 Contemporary Music Festival in Oberlin, Ohio.

Wilson is familiar with traditional forms. His music, however, speaks of the present. In his use of complex rhythms, atonal harmonies, intervallic concepts and cacophonous undertakings, he dwells on penetrating settings of contemporary moods.

Among his works are *Prelude and Line Study* for woodwind quartet; *Trio for Flute, Cello and Piano; Two Dutch Poems; Structure for Orchestra; String Quartet; Wry Fragments, Tenor and Percussion Ensemble; Violin Sonata; Gloria for a cappella chorus; Dance Suite; Soliloquy* for bass viol; *And Death Shall Have No Dominion* for tenor and percussion ensemble; *Sextet; Three Movements for Orchestra; Chanson Innocent* for contralto and two bassoons; *Dance Music II; Piece for Four; Biography* (Leroi Jones); *Cetus; In Memoriam Martin Luther King, Jr.,* for chorus and electronic sounds; *Piano Piece* for piano and electronic sounds; *Orchestral Piece* and others.

STEPHEN CHAMBERS (1940-   )

Stephen Chambers, a composer born in Asheville, North Carolina, currently lives in New York. Having been educated at the Manhattan School of Music, at the New York College of Music and the New School for Social Research, he has studied privately with Robert Starer, William Sydeman, Hall Overton, David Reck, Morton Feldman, Chou Wen-Chung, Charles Whittenberg and Ornette Coleman.

His works have enjoyed various performances throughout the United States, but mostly in New York City. From 1965 to the present time, his works have been presented on *Music in Our Time* over the YMHA radio station at the ASCAP Composers' Showcase in 1965 in a joint concert with the Ornette Coleman Trio-Quarter and the Philadelphia Woodwind Quintet in 1967, to mention a few. A composer worth noting, his music currently is in regular demand.

Chambers serves as lecturer and panelist on various occasions, such as the Music Workshop in Harlem in 1968, and at Hofstra University in 1968. He also served as conductor-panelist at other programs and conferences. Other honors have been received from ASCAP. He is a cofounder and first vice-president of the Society of Black Composers, a recently formed group of New York composers. Chambers has written a book of first poems, released by Fro-Arts, and has generally maintained a level of continuous involvement in the field of fine music.

Of his music, he has this to say: "I write Black contemporary music in all musical idioms and forms". Chambers uses elements from rock to art music in contemporary techniques to create a spontaniety of style and imagination. Basically a believer in the fact that music must bear likeness to the lifestyles of Blacks and their environment, his music bears slight similarities to a jazz format. Although various linear characteristics punctuate his works, the main emphasis is intervallic construction with total "sound image."

Among his compositions are the following: *Elements* for violin, viola, flute, clarinet, cello, piano, glass and bamboo, winds and chimes; *Quote-Unquote* for bass-baritone, oboe, trumpet, 2 percussion; *Sound-gone* for piano; *Roots and Other Things; Moments; Contours; Shapes for Chamber Orchestra; Titles,* for woodwind quartet; *Portraits* for alto flute, bass clarinet, 3 percussion and piano; *Three Play Short Five* for double bass, percussion, bass clarinet; *Four* for clarinet, trumpet, trombone and piano; *Encounter; Six Players and a Voice; Duo* for flute and clarinet; *Song-Short; Sketches* for brass quintet; *Sound-Images* for 3 percussion, string bass, 3 brass, 6 female voices; *Inner-Sections;* and others.

Many other composers from the Black Society of Composers, from free-lance statuses and various institutions are not represented here. Vada Butcher has published a manual to include contemporary composers unknown to the general public; a few recordings have recently been released to include newer faces; and also indicative of the numbers of Black composers is the long list of 300 names issued by the Indiana Symposiums on Black Composers. Among those talents noted are Dorothy Rudd Moore, William Fischer, Reginald Parker, Leonard de Paur, James Frazier, Walter Anderson, Joseph Hayes, Roger Dickerson, Ralph Simpson, Gilbert Allen, Julia Perry, Charles Jones, John Duncan, Orville Moseley, Daniel Owens, and others. There is also an ever-growing list of newer composers such as Percy Gregory, William Moore, Harvey Van Buren and Eugene Simpson, who with established ones, carry the message and philosophy of identity, change and musical freedom, together with a knowledge of the world about them. Their talents are equally varied, imaginative, artistic and perceptive. And while this book cannot review the fine accomplishments of each composer, it nevertheless points out the great varieties of musical talents found in the contemporary era.

XV
THE FUTURE:
ART MUSIC VERSUS POPULAR MUSIC?

Society today not only poses some questions concerning the right to compose within certain forms and techniques, but also questions the best available medium of expression for this Black identity. Should Black composers be restricted to forms or techniques generally associated with traditionally Black forms? Or should composers merge with the period in which they live and participate in all existing elements of music? Should music rise above the faction of society which debases or criticizes by types and people, or should music be left for all to enjoy? What is the future of Black music, and what was its past? Can Black music be identified as that of Afro-Americans? Is there Black music at all? And finally, what music is representative of both the Afro-American whose heritage is African and whose citizenship is, by birth, American? The final chapter will ponder these questions and discuss the nature of survival of both the Black society and its music.

Many Blacks have felt that Black art musicians were traitors to a Black heritage. They knew nothing of Elizabeth Greenfield, Blind Thomas Bethune and George Bridgetower, or of Chevalier de Saint Georges or of the countless others who had pioneered in art music long before the era of jazz. On the other hand, few in art music knew of Tom Turpin, Jelly Roll Morton and Scott Joplin.

White Americans once voiced another opinion of the matter. Their actions stated that Black folk musicians were acceptable as entertainers, and that art musicians were almost acceptable as vocalists. They also showed that the efforts of art musicians could not possibly be taken seriously and felt that Blacks should simply restrict their activities to popular music. Whereas Black critics felt that Black composers should develop their own music such as jazz, Whites simply considered them too inferior to practice concert or art music. Blacks, they said, were designed to improvise, to make "fun music" for brothels. But to participate in composing, conducting or performing art music was unthinkable for the majority of Black Americans. They became victims of this propaganda.

The social conditions and biased associations led to a frustration and ambivalence in the practice of both popular music and art music. Some practiced popular music because they wanted to; others, because they had to. While popular musicians worked continuously and received ready fame and fortune, art music composers were generally neglected. For the latter, publishers abandoned their causes, while promoting music by popular composers. Blacks led no orchestras, performed in no symphonies, performed no significant concerts at the institutions of higher learning, and produced few recordings of their works. No one realized the potential of Black Americans, not even they themselves.

Consequently, many composers became greatly disillusioned with America and traveled to Europe in order to seek a more respectable existence and an appreciation of their talents. Others trained in art music took up the practice of jazz and accomplished sound developments in the then non-established form. Significantly, still others remained in America and wrote in both types simultaneously.

The fact now, however, is that popular music and art music enjoy a healthy competition and are worthy of the accolades extended them. Never before has the world of art music given as much thought to popular music as today, and never more credit, study, and bold admission of the comradeship between the two. Popular music has even grown so strong as to boast superiority, particularly as far as jazz is concerned. This is especially true since trained musicians are not restricting their talents to one medium alone. It is now more common for musicians to practice professionally in both the academic and popular forms at once.

The contemporary period offers many choices, styles and philosophies concerning popular and art music forms. Many feel that jazz and other popular forms have reached parity with the traditional classical music, and that they will either merge in complexity or will become the epitome of simplicity. Others feel that jazz is the real classical music of Blacks, and of America. Based upon the traditional history related above, society, they say, has led Blacks to seek a more separate art as approved by a Black definition. And even according to the definitions already established, some feel that jazz fits the concept of "classical music". For example, jazz has withstood the "test of time", concerning itself with decorum in performance, with ornamentation, improvisation and nuances common to the pleasant aesthetics and professional achievements of music. In addition, art music has benefited by its innumerable experiments from instrumental ranges and stamina to a compositional technique. Jazz has also abandoned the sole function of dance music, and has attained the rank of "music for listening" and analysis. Still others feel that both are so inbred that there is no need to separate them. They feel that the history of both classical and popular music has consisted of enough Black contributions to allow them to claim any participation within any type of music. These musicians point to parallelism of techniques, evaluation in functions and plagiarism. In some cases, both types become inseparable and are not easily distinguishable. Both have evolved from Africa. Both have enjoyed active and passive participation from their listeners. Yet both are on the verge of becoming extinct unless a more definitive clarification evolves between third streamism, avant-garde, or some other concept. While art music and jazz are not the same, many characteristics and similarities are apparent. To further contribute to the confusion, many jazz performers have admitted to being impressed with Stravinsky, Bach and other classicists. Yet Stravinsky is reported to have been equally fascinated with jazz.

The real definitions and prognosis of popular music, art music or Black music are not easy, for there is a history of excellence in all types of music. Few can tell twelve-tone jazz from twelve-tone art music or without previous study, the music of Hale Smith from that of a White counterpart using the same compositional techniques. Few can distinguish whether a composer better loves his well-planned rock-opera or his classical opera since equal efforts are used to create both. Yet composers themselves have less trouble explaining the music around them (i.e., the style, type and future). To them, the future rests in any medium of expression which they choose. Their music is life itself — what they see and know, and what they experience and do. They demand the freedom to compose as they wish and demand the freedom for rivalry and coexistence among all musical forms. Most composers do not like restrictions, but relish versatility. One composer, Arthur Cunningham, who has written numerous works from orchestral pieces to rock, uses a descriptive poem to denote a general feeling among contemporary composers. His thoughts give a potential cue to the future of music.

LET OTHERS DREAM

What they Dream
I Dream
Music

I am a source person
My body
Its height width length and color
Is my house

The earth
My estate
The universe
My place

Call me what you will
Call my music
MUSIC

Arthur Cunningham
(Used by permission)

The future of Afro-American music is supported by its past, and depends upon this heritage for its future survival. Reflected in a long history of oral tradition, improvisation, harmonic variety and rhythmic perfection, this music enjoys a certain unique characteristic in its performance and acceptability of popular and folk forms. But never has the contribution toward such intellectual aesthetics been rewarded for its astuteness, practicality and beauty. Black composers have practiced their music in many types of compositions and philosophies, only now commanding the just respect which they deserve. Perhaps this knowledge of the past, this completeness of characteristic styles and a forward movement will guarantee an acceptance of individual talents, forms and ideas, and will render a new performance for tomorrow.

But knowledge and acceptance of Black music, no matter what its definition, semantics and interchange, will not be effected without the benefit of concerned Americans. Black music should be promoted, learned, studied, probed and considered as being American. All should invest in the enrichment of these compositions through performance and listening experiences. Publishers and recording industries must join with the public to support the heritage of a music which is interwoven with American tradition and whose message for all minds speaks of freedom now!

Fig. 28. Map of modern Africa.

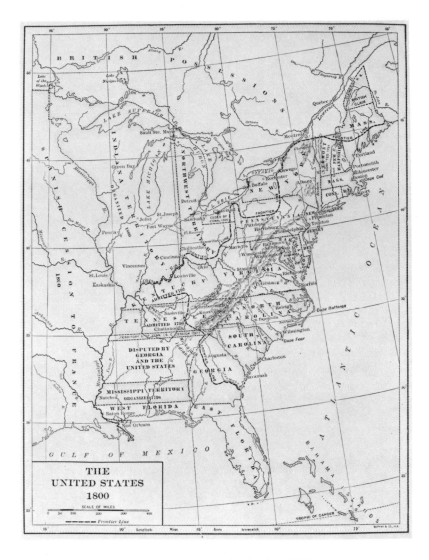

Fig. 29. Map of America in the 1800's.

READINGS AND RECORDINGS

Chapter I: Historical Background

Aptheker, Herbert. *American Negro Slave Revolts*. New York: Columbia University, 1943.

Bennett, Lerone, Jr. *Before the Mayflower: A History of the Negro in America from 1619-1964*. Baltimore: Penguin Books, 1968.

Botkin, B. A. *Lay My Burden Down*. Chicago: University of Chicago Press. 1968.

Butcher, Margaret. *Negro in the American Culture*. New York: Alfred Knopf, 1969.

Davidson, Basil. *The African Past*. New York: Atlantic-Little Brown.

Dubois, W. E. B. *The Souls of Black Folk*. New York: Avon Books, 1965.

Elkins, Stanley. *Slavery: A Problem in American Institutional and Intellectual Life*. Chicago: University of Chicago Press, 1969.

Franklin, John Hope. "Brief History of the Negro in the United States". *American Negro Reference Book*. Englewood Cliffs: Prentice-Hall, 1966.

————. *From Slavery to Freedom*. New York: Alfred Knopf, 1948.

Frazier, E. Franklin. *The Negro in the United States*. New York: Macmillan, 1957.

Graham, Gerald, ed. *McLean of the Gold Coast*. Lindon: Oxford Univ. Press, 1962.

Hayes, William. *Most Ancient Egypt*. Chicago: University of Chicago, 1965.

Jones, Leroi. *Blues People*. New York: Apollo, 1968.

Snowden, Frank. *Blacks in Antiquity*. Cambridge: Belnap-Harvard, 1970.

Supplementary: Slave Narratives by Josiah Henson, Sojourner Truth, Lunceford Lane and Others.

Recordings: *A Portrait of the Black Man, Sidney Portier Reads*. Victor.

Chapter II: African Heritage

Historical

Bohsnan, Paul. *Africa and Africans*. Natural History Press. 1964.

Bowdich, Edward. *Mission From Cape Coast Castle to Ashanti*. London.

Coughlan, Robert. *Tropical Africa,* Life World Library, New York Time, 1963.

Howard, C. and Plumb, J. H., eds. *West African Explorers*. London: Oxford University Press, 1951.

Jobson, Richard. *The Golden Trade*. London: Oxford University Press, 1623.

Lincoln, Eric. *A Pictorial History of the Negro.* New York: Crown.

MacMichael, H. A. *A History of the Arabs in the Sudan.* Volume I. London: Frank Cass and Company, 1967.

Oliver, Roland, ed. *Dawn of African History.* London: Oxford University Press, 1968.

———. ed. *The Middle Age of African History.* London: Oxford University Press, 1967.

Seligman, C. G. *Races of Africa.* New York: Oxford University Press, 1967.

Woldering, Irmgard. *The Art of Egypt.* New York: Greystone Press, 1963.

Musical

Aning, B. A. "Factors That Shape and Maintain Folk Music in Ghana". *Journal of International Folk Music Council.* Volume XX, 1968.

Baines, A. *Musical Instruments Through the Ages.* London: Penguin, 1961.

Coughlan, Robert. *Tropical Africa.* New York: Time Inc., 1963.

Dietz, Betty and Olatunji, Michael. *Musical Instruments of Africa.* New York: John Day, 1965.

Geis, Darlene and Kittler, Glenn. *Nigeria and Ghana.* New York: Children Press, 1962.

Jones, A. M. *Africa and Indonesia: The Evidence of the Xylophone and Other Musical and Cultural Factors.* London: E. J. Brill, 1959.

———. *Studies in African Music,* Volumes I and II. London: Oxford University Press, 1959.

Makeba, Miriam. *The World of African Songs.* Chicago: Quadrangle, 1971.

Marfurt, Luitfud. *Musik in Afrika.* Nymphenburger, 1957.

Nettl, Bruno. *Music in Primitive Culture.* Cambridge: Harvard University Press, 1956.

Nketia, J. Kwabena. *African Music in Ghana.* Illinois: Northwestern Press.

———. *Drumming in Akan Communities of Ghana.* Edinburg: Thomas Nelson and Sons, 1963.

———. *Folk Songs of Ghana.* London: Oxford University Press, 1963.

———. *Music in Ghana.* London: Longmans Green, 1962.

———. "Musicology and African Music: A Review of Problems and Areas of Study". *Africa and the Wider World.* London: Brokensha and Crowder, eds.

———. "The Problem of Meaning in African Music". *Ethnomusicology.* Volume IV, No. 3, 1960.

———. *Our Drums and Drummers.* Accra: Ghana Publishing House, 1968.

———. "The Hocket Technique in African Music". *Journal of the International Folk Music Council.* Volume, XIV, 1962.

Opuku, A. M. *African Dances.* Leon: African Institute, University of Ghana.

Sachs, Curt. *History of Musical Instruments.* New York, 1940.

———. *Rise of Music in the Ancient World, East and West.* New York: Norton, 1934.

184

Wachsmann, Klaus. "Essays on Music and History in Africa and Asia." Royal Anthropological Institute for Great Britain and North Ireland. London.

———. "The Trend of Musicology in Africa." *Institute of Ethnomusicology.* University of California, Volume I, No. 1, Los Angeles.

Wallaschek, Richard. *Primitive Music.* London: Longsman, 1893.

Warren, Fred and Lee. *The Music of Africa.* Englewood Cliffs: Prentice Hall, Inc. 1970.

Waterman, Richard. "African Influence on American Negro Music" in Soltax ed. *Acculturation in the Americas,* Chicago: University of Chicago Press, 1947.

Wilson, Margaret Welch, ed. *Our African Neighbors.* Gastonia: Brumley.

Recordings

Africa: *Musical Instruments, Textiles, Jewelry and Architecture.* filmstrip with recordings. Warren Schloat Productions, Inc. Pleasantville: 1969.

African Society's Best Music for 1952. Decca: LF1171, No. 6.

Anthology of Music of Black Africa. Everest Records: EV3254/3.

Folkways Recordings. Library of Congress.

Ghana Asuafo Reto Dwom. University of Ghana Chorus. Request Records.

The Music of Africa Today. U. Art. UAS. 15556.

Makeba, Miriam. RCA Victor LPM2267; and Reprise 6274.

Oluntuji, Michael. *Drums of Passion.*

Chapters III and IV: Early Folk Songs and Spirituals

Historical

Douglass, Frederick. *My Bondage and My Freedom.* New York: 1853.

Drimmer, Melvin. *Black History, A Reappraisal.* New York: Doubleday.

Herskovits, Milville. *The Myth of the Negro Past.* New York: Beacon.

Hughes, Langston and Meltzer, Milton. *Black Magic: A Pictorial History of the Negro in American Entertainment.* Englewood Cliffs: Prentice-Hall, 1967.

Musical

Allen, W. F., Garrison, Lucy and Ware, C. P. *Slave Songs of the United States.* New York: Simpson and Company. 1867.

Bontemps, Arna. *American Negro Poetry.* New York: American Century and Long. 1963.

Burleigh, Harry T. *Minstrel Melodies.* New York; Schirmer, 1886.

———. *Negro Spirituals.* New York: Franco Colombo.

Courlander, Harold. *Negro Folk Music, U.S.A.* Chicago: Chicago University Press, 1963.

Epstein, Dena. "Slave Music in the U.S. Before 1860." *Notes* Spring, 2963.

Fischer, Miles. *Negro Slave Songs in the U.S.* New York: Russell and Russell, 1968.

George, Zelma. "Negro Music in American Life." *The American Negro Reference Book.* J. Davis, ed. Englewood Cliffs: Prentice-Hall, 1966.

Hare, Maud Cuney. *Negro Musicians and Their Music.* Washington: Associated Press. 1936.

Hughes, Langston and Bontemps, Arna. *The Book of Negro Folklore.* New York: Dodd, Mead and Company, 1958.

Hughes, Langston. *Famous Negro Music Makers.* New York: Dodd, Mead and Company, 1955.

Jahn, Janheinz. *Negro Spirituals.* Fischer-Bucherei, 1962.

      . *Blues Und Work Songs.* Fischer-Bucherei.

Jackson, George. (White) *Spiritual Folk Songs of Early America.* New York: Dover, 1937.

Johnson, James W. and J. Rosamond. *The Book of Negro Spirituals.* Volumes I and II. New York: Viking Press, 1969.

Krehbiel, H. E. *Afro-American Folksongs.* New York: Schirmer, 1914.

Landeck, Beatrice. *Echoes of Africa.* New York: McKay and Company, 1969.

Lomax, John and Alan. *Folk Song U.S.A.* New York: Duell, Sloan and Pierce.

      . *Ballads of America.* New York: MacMillan, 1953.

Locke, Alain. *The Negro and His Music.*

Lowens, Irving. *Music and Musicians in Early America.* New York: W. W. Norton, 1964.

Pichierri, Louis. *Music in New Hampshire,* 1623-1800. New York: Columbia University Press, 1960.

Stevenson, Rober. "Afro-American Legacy to 1800". *Musical Quarterly,* October, 1968.

Toppin, Edgar. *A Mark Well Made.* Chicago: Rand McNally, 1967.

White, Clarence Cameron. *Negro Folk Melodies.*

White, Newman. *American Negro Folk Music, U.S.A.* Haddon-Croft, 1965.

Work, John. *American Negro Songs.* New York: Bonanza, 1940, (See other collections by Dett, Bond, Jessye, Cook and H. Johnson)

Recordings

Boatwright McHenry *Sings Spirituals,* Atlantic: RE7024.

Botkin, B. A. *Folk Music of the United States.* Library of Congress. AAFSL10.

Courlander, Harold. Folkways, Volume I. *Negro Folk Music of Alabama.*

Elan, Dorothy. *Historical Interpretation of Negro Spirituals* and *Lift Every Voice and Sing.* Camden: Franklin Publishing Company.

Hayes, Roland Sings Spirituals.

Johnson, James W. *New Born Again.* Film with selections from *God's Trombones.*

Lomax, Alan. Folk Music of the United States. Library of Congress: AAFS L30; The *Ballad Hunter,* AAFS-L49. *Blues and Gospel Songs* AAFS-L3; *Blues and Game Songs,* AAFS-L4.

Price, Leontyne Sings Spirituals.

Robeson, Paul Sings Spirituals.

Stracke, W. and Hurt, O. *Black Folk Music in America*: filmstrip with recordings. Burton Munk and Company, 1970.

Others: *Spirituals* by Tuskegee Institute Choir, Fisk Jubilee Singers, Hampton Institute, Virginia State College and others.

Chapters V and VI: Historical Background and Black Minstrels

Historical

Bennett, Lerone. *Before the Mayflower.* Baltimore: Penguin, 1964, 1962.

Franklin, John H. *From Slavery to Freedom.* New York, 1947.

Johnson, James W. *The Autobiography of an Ex-Colored Man.* New York, 1965.

Lynch, John Roy. *The Facts of Reconstruction.* New York, 1913.

Murray, Pauli. *Laws on Race and Color.* Cincinnati, 1951.

Washington, Booker T. *Up From Slavery.* New York, 1901.

Musical

Boni, Margaret. *Fireside Book of Folk Songs.* New York: Simon Schuster, 1974.

Burleigh, H. T. *Minstrel Melodies.* New York: Schirmer, 1886.

Callender's Original Colored Minstrel Songster. 1882.

Daly, John. *A Song in His Heart.* Philadelphia: J. Winston, 1955.

Day, Charles. *Fun in Black.* Dewitt, 1874.

Ewen, David. *History of Popular Music.* New York: Barnes and Nole, 1961.

————. *The Life and Death of Tin Pan.* New York: Funk and Wagnalls, 1964.

Goldberg, Isaac. *Tin Pan Alley.* New York: J. Day, 1930.

Haywood, Charles, ed. *James Bland Album.* New York: Edward B. Marks, 1946.

Howard, John T. and Bellows, George. *Music in America.* New York: Crowell, 1957.

Lomax, J. and Alan. *American Ballads and Folk Songs.* New York: MacMillan, 1953.

Nathan, Hans. *Dan Emmett and the Rise of Early Negro Minstrelsy,* 1910.

Niane, D. T. *Sundiata: An Expic of Old Mali.* Humanities Press, 1969.

Paskman, Dailey. *Gentlemen, Be Seated.* 1928.

Patterson, Lindsey. "The Negro in Music and Art." *Encyclopedia on Negro History and Art.* Volume IX. Washington: Associated Press.

Scarborough, Dorothy. *On the Trail of Negro Folk Songs.* Cambridge: Harvard University Press, 1925.

Scott, John Anthony. *The Ballad of America: The History of the United States.* Bantam, 1966.

Speath, Sigmund. *History of Popular Music in America.* New York: Random House, 1948.

Wittke, Carl. *Tambo and Mr. Bones.* New York: Edward B. Marks, 1829.

Recordings

Debussy, Claude. *Golliwog's Cakewalk.*

Gentlemen Be Seated. Epic Records LN 3596. arr. and conducted by B. Masingill.

Chapters VII, VIII and IX: Jazz: Forms, Styles and Composers

Historical

Aptheker, Herbert. *Documentary History of the Negro People in the United States.* 1951.

Cotner, Robert; Ezell, John; and Fite, Gilbert. *Readings in American History,* Volume II. Boston: Houghton Mifflin, 1952.

Frazier, Franklin. *The Negro in the United States.* New York: MacMillan, 1957.

Wish, Harvey. *The Negro Since Emancipation.* 1958.

Musical

Asch, Moses and Lomax, Alan. *The Leadbelly Songbook,* New York: Oak, 1962.

Armstrong, Louis. *My Life in New Orleans.* New York: Prentice-Hall.

Baker, David. *Jazz Improvisation.* Chicago: Maher, 1969.

Blesh, Rudi and Janis, Harriet. *They All Played Ragtime.* New York:

Blesh, Rudi and Janis, Harriet. *They All Played Ragtime.* New York: Knopf, 1960.

Bruynoghe, Yannick. *Big Bill Blues.* New York: Oak, 1964.

Charters, Ann. *Ragtime Songbook.* New York: Oak, 1965.

Charters, Samuel. *Jazz: New Orleans.* New York: Oak, 1963.

Copland, Aaron. "Jazz Structure and Influence." *Modern Music.* 4:9-14. January-February, 1927.

————. *The New Music.* New York: W. W. Norton, 1968.

De Toledano, Ralph, ed. *Frontiers of Jazz.* New York: Unger, 1962.

Dexter, Dave, Jr. *Jazz Calvacade: The Inside Story of Jazz.* Criterion, 1946.

Edwards, A. and Marrocco, W. T. *Music in the United States.* Dubuque: William Brown, 1968.

Erlich, Lillian. *What Jazz Is All About.* New York: Messner, 1966.

Feather, Leonard. *Encyclopedia of Jazz.* New York: Bonanza, 1962.

————. *Inside Bebop.* New York: Robbins, 1949.

Gershwin, George. "The Relation of Jazz to American Music". *American Composers on American Music.* Stanford University Press, 1933.

Handy, W. C. *Father of the Blues.* New York: Collier, 1941.

Hodeir, Andre. *Jazz: Its Evolution and Essence.* New York: Grove, 1956.

Keil, Charles. *Urban Blues.* Chicago: University of Chicago Press, 1969.

Keepnews, Orrin and Graver, B. *A Pictorial History of Jazz.* Crown, 1966.

Martin, John and Fritz, William. *Listening to Jazz.* Fresno: University of Fresno Press, 1970.

Mehegan, John. *Jazz Improvisation,* Volumes I-IV. New York: Watson-Guptil, 1962.

Meyer, Sheldon. *The Story of Jazz.* New York: Grosset and Dunlap, 1960.

Mezzrow, Milton and Wolfe, Bernard. *Really the Blues.* New York: Random House, 1946.

Morath, Max. *Giants of Ragtime.* New York: Ed. B. Marks, 1971.

Pleasants, Henry. *Serious Music and All That Jazz.* New York: Simon Schuster, 1969.

Rose, Al and Souchon, Emond. *New Orleans Jazz*. Louisiana: State University Press, 1967.

Shapiro, Nat and Hentoff, Nat. *Hear Me Talkin' to Ya'*. New York: Rinehart, 1955.

. *The Jazz Makers*. New York: Grove, 1958.

Silverman, Jerry. *Folk Blues*. New York: Oak, 1958.

Stearns, Marshall. *The Story of Jazz*. New York: MacMillan, 1968.

Tanner, Paul 'and Gerow, Maurice. *A Study of Jazz*. Dubuque: William Brown, 1964.

Ulanov, Barry. *A History of Jazz in America*. New York: Viking, 1952.

Waters, Ethel. *His Eye Is on the Sparrow*. New York: Doubleday, 1951.

Williams, Martin. *Jazz Masters of New Orleans*. New York: MacMillan, 1967.

, ed. *The Art of Jazz*. New York: Oxford, 1959.

Others: Afro-American Newspaper; *Clavier* Keyboard; Vol. IX, No. 7, Oct. 1970: *Ebony* Magazine; *BMI* and *Downbeat* Magazines.

Recordings

Bernstein, Leonard. *Jazz Concerto*.

Milhaud, Darius. *La Creation*. RCA Victor LD 2625.

Stravinsky, Igor. *Ragtime for Eleven Instruments*.

Armstrong, Louis. *Hello Dolly; Weather Bird; Hot Five & Seven* albums.

Davis, Miles. *Birth of the Cool*. Capitol DT-1974.

Ellington, Duke, and His Orchestra. "Nutcracker", etc. Columbia: 32160252: also Decca 79224: *Ellington Era:* CL2046.

Essays in Ragtime. Folkways FG3563.

Franklin, Aretha. *Lady Soul*. Atlantic SC 8176.

Garner, Erroll. *Early Erroll*. Columbia J1269: also *Concert By the Sea*. CL 883.

Gillespie, Dizzy, and His Band. Crescendo 23.

Harris, Bill. *Caught in the Act*. Als E. Marcy 36097.

Jazz. Folkways.

Jazz Omnibus. Columbia. CL 1020.

Joplin, Scott. *Jazz*, Vol. 11. Folkways FP75, side 2; also: *Piano Rags*, Rifkin, pianist, Nonesuch H 71248.

Monk, Thelonius. *Monk's Music*, Riverside, RLP 12-242.

Morton, Jelly Roll, Recordings of, w/Eubie Blake, James Johnson, et al: Folkways FG 3563 (see *Essays*).

Parker, Charlie. Fantasy 6011.

Powell, Bud, The Amazing. Blue Note BLP 1598: also *Bud's Mood*. Verve MGV-8154.

Taylor, Billy. *Trio*. Volumes I & II. Prestige 7015, 7016.

Waller, Fats. *Handful of Keys*. RCA Victor: LPM1502.

Williams, Mary Lou. *Zodiac Suite*. Verve VRS6024.

Chapter X: Art Music

Apel, Willi. *Harvard Dictionary of Music*. Cambridge: Harvard University Press, 1958.

Brawley, Benjamin. *The Negro Genius.* Bible and Tanner.

Butcher, Margaret. *Negro in the American Culture.* New York; Knopf, 1969.

Grout, Donald. *History of Music in Western Civilization.* New York: Schirmer, 1958.

Ewen, David. *American Composers Today.* H. W. Wilson and Company, 1949.

Hare, Maud Cuney. *Negro Musicians and Their Music.* Washington: Associated Press, 1936.

Machlis, Joseph. *Introduction to Contemporary Music.* New York: W. W. Norton, 1961.

Miller, Hugh Milton. *History of Music.* New York: Barnes and Noble, 1968.

Patterson, Lindsey: "The Negro in Music and Art." *Encyclopedia of Negro History and Art.* Volume IX. Washington: Associated Press.

Recordings

Dawson, William. *Negro Folk Symphony.* Decca DL 10077.

Kay, Ulysses. *Brass Quartet. Folk Ways: Choral Triptych, Cambridge Records; Round Dance and Polka.* CRI 209; *Choral Works.* Cambridge CRM 416; *Serenade for Orchestra.* Louisville Philharmonic Special: LOU 545-8.

Music of Black Composers, Natalie Hinderas, pianist, Music of Dett, Work and Still. Desto DC 7102-3.

Still, William Grant. *Afro-American Symphony.* MI118.

Swanson, Howard. *Night Music.* Decca DCM 3215; *Seven Songs,* Desto B432; *Short Symphony.* American Recording Society: ARS7.

Chapters XI-XV: Historical Background:
Contemporary: Jazz: and New Music

Historical

Addison, Gyle, ed. *The Black Aesthetic.* New York: Doubleday, 1971.

Brown, Claude. *Manchild in the Promised Land.*

Carmichael, Stokely. *Black Power.*

Fanon, Frantz. *The Wretched of the Earth.* New York: Grave Press, 1968.

Kenyatta, Jomo. *Toward Mt. Kenya.* Knopf.

King, Martin Luther. *I Have A Dream.*

        . *Stride Toward Freedom.*

Lincoln, Eric. *Black Muslims in America.*

Malcolm X. *Autobiography.*

Also *Downbeat; BMI Music Journal; Ebony.* Current newspapers.

Recordings

Black Composer in America, The. Desto DC 7107.

Coltrane, John. *A Love Supreme.* Impulse A77.

Coleman, Ornette. *The Art of Improvisers.* Atlantic SD1572; *Free Jazz.*

Jones, Quincy. *Walking in Space.* AM3023; Mercury Records & Reprive.

Lewis, John and Asmussen.

Music of Black Composers; (Walker, Cunningham and Smith, Chambers) Natalie Hinderas, pianist. Desto DC 7102-3.

Smith, Hale. *Nuances.* Sam Fox Publishing Company.

Sowande, Fela. Tape N543.26/7. Broadcasting Foundation of America. N. Y.

Wilson, Olly. *Electronic Music,* Volume IV, Turnabout Recordings; TV 34301; *In Memoriam Martin Luther King,* Oberlin, 1968-69.

Trio Pro Viva. *Contemporary Black Images.* T & T Associates. Raleigh.

LIST OF MUSICAL TERMS

A cappella — unaccompanied vocal music.
Adagio — slow speed.
Ad libitum — at will of performer; freedom to interpret.
Air — simple melody or tune.
Allegro — lively speed; spirited.
Andante — walking or moderate speed.
Aria — a melody or air in an opera, oratorio, etc.
Arpeggio — broken chord tones.
Art song — a vocal air, aria, etc.
Atonal — without key emphasis.
Ballet — piece for dancers and orchestral accompaniment.
Bar — measure.
Bar line — vertical division between measures.
Binary form — two-part piece, usually with repeats.
Break — instrumental interlude in jazz compositions.
Cadence — ending.
Cantata — a large work for voices.
Chamber music — that written for small ensembles.
Chord — two or more tones played together.
Chromatic — distance of a half-step.
Combo — small ensemble.
Composer — one who writes and/or conceives music by originality and inspiration.
Concerto — piece containing several movements of varying speeds, for solo and orchestral accompaniment.
Consonant — agreement; chordal.
Classical — term describing both the music of the late 18th century and a general type based on intellectual affiliation.
Contrapuntal — characterized by counterpoint; melody against melody.
Contrary motion — melodies or harmonies in opposing directions.
Counterpoint — note against note; contrapuntal.
Development — middle section of sonata-allegro or first movement.
Diatonic — stepwise or scalewise.
Dissonant — harsh, non-traditional blendings.
Dynamics — symbols used to indicate loudness or softness.
Ensemble — group of players; together.
Element — constituent or part; substance of composition.
Etude — study piece emphasizing a technical difficulty.
Exposition — first section of Sonata-allegro movement.
Form — shape or structure of composition.
Forte — loud.

Fugue — imitative piece employing specific rules for voice entrances; based on same theme throughout.

Glissando — gliding or sliding across successive tones.

Grave — slow speed.

Half step — smallest unit between two tones; chromatic.

Harmony — science of sound; agreement, togetherness; chordal.

Heritage — that handed down by one's ancestors, as culture, tradition or birthright.

Homophony — chordal, having predominant melody.

Imitation — repetition of theme or part by other voices.

Interval — distance.

Inversion — mirror-like exchange of intervals or melody; upside down.

Jam session — jazz group performing in usually spontaneous way.

Key — tone, note or scale.

Keynote — tonic or main tonal emphasis.

Largo — very slow.

Lento — slow.

Linear — melodic.

Liturgical — of the church; religious ritual.

Major scale — eight notes in succession, having half-steps between third and fourth tones and seventh and eighth.

Mass — liturgical order of worship in celebration of Last Supper.

Measure — quantity of metric equality, divided by bar lines.

Melody — tune, theme, primary linear or horizontal arrangement of individual tones.

Meter — numerical signature for relationships between notes and their durations of sound.

Medium — means by which a composition is performed; instrument scored.

Movement — section of piece determined by speed, key and form.

Monody — single line or melodic element; unison.

Minuet — dance in three.

Mode — type of scale or quality of intervals such as major or minor.

Motive — theme or melody.

Note — key, pitch, tone.

Octet — piece for eight players, usually containing movements.

Opera — music drama, predominantly vocal with orchestral accompaniment.

Oratorio — piece composed of ensemble and solo parts, usually of religious theme.

Orchestration — compositional writing for instruments.

Overture — opening piece.

Parallel — similar motion.

Phrase — musical sentence.

Piano — soft.

Polyphony — many sounds; melodies in imitative counterpoint.

Polytonal — many keys used simultaneously.

Pitch — key, note.

Presto — very fast and lively speed.

Prelude — opening piece.

Quartet — piece designed for four players, usually containing several movements.

Quintet — piece designed for five players, usually containing several movements.

Recapitulation — last section of a sonata-allegro movement; return of main themes.

Rest — symbol equivalent to silent duration of a note.

Requiem — mass for the dead.

Retrograde — crab motion or backward order of tone row.

Rhythm — pulsation or flow of music; movement.

Row — atonal melody based on serial or twelve-tone technique.

Scale — successive, diatonic movement in given orders.

Scherzo — playful piece.

Score — music written down.

Sextet — piece written for six players, usually having several movements.

Septet — piece for seven players, usually with several movements.

Seventh — chord composed of four tones, built in thirds.

Solo — piece for one performer.

Sonata — "sound piece" consisting of several movements contrasting in mood, key and form.

Strophic — piece with different verses set to same music.

Subject — theme or main melody.

Suite — piece containing several movements with dance characteristics.

Syncopation — displacement of the expected rhythmic schemes.

Symphony — piece written for orchestra containing several movements.

Tempo — speed.

Theme — motive, subject or main melody.

Third — interval composed of a distance of three notes apart.

Timbre — characteristic quality of instrumental or vocal sound.

Time signature — meter found at the beginning of composition indicating predominant note value.

Toccata — touch piece employing flashy technical characteristics and fantasy-like features.

Tonal — emphasis of key or scale.

Tonic — keynote.

Triad — chord composed of three notes.

Trio — piece for three players, usually in sonata form.

Tune — melody or theme.

Twelve tone — chromatic or serial music.

Unison — same melody in all parts.

Vivace — quick and lively.

Waltz — dance in three.

Whole step — scale-wise interval composed of two half steps.

CHRONOLOGICAL LIST OF COMPOSERS AND PUBLISHERS

Anglo-Africans

1779–1860   Bridgetower, George Augustus Polgren: Indiana U.

1875–1912   Coleridge-Taylor, Samuel: Novello; Augener; Schirmer.

Afro-Americans

1848–1916   Lucas, Samuel: Oliver Ditson; Theodore Presser, Pa.

1849–1908   Bethune, Thomas (Blind Tom): Schirmer, N.Y.

1854–1911   Bland, James: Schirmer, N.Y.

1866–1949   Burleigh, Henry (Harry) T.: Franco Colombo, N.Y.

1868–1917   Joplin, Scott: Stark; E. B. Marks, N.Y.

1869–1954   Freeman, Harry L.: Pace-Handy, N.Y.

1869–1944   Cook, Marion C.: Schirmer, N.Y.

1873–1958   Handy, William C.: Handy Brothers, N.Y.

1873–1954   Johnson, J. Rosamond: Edward B. Marks, N.Y.

1873–1922   Turpin, Thomas: Edward B. Marks, N.Y.

1880–1960   White, Clarence Cameron: Summy-Birchard, Evanston.

1881–1946   Brymn, Tim: Folkways Recordings.

1882–1943	Dett, Robert Nathaniel: Summy-Birchard, Evanston.
1883–	Blake, Hubert (Eubie): Edward B. Marks, N.Y.
1883–1958	Dabney, Ford: Folkways Recordings.
1885-1941	Morton, Ferdinand (Jelly Roll):
1888–1970	Johnson, Hall: Robbins; Fisher, N.Y.
1888–1953	Price, Florence: Affiliated Musicians, Los Angeles.
1891–1955	Johnson, James P.: Belwin Mills, N.Y.
1895–	Still, William Grant: Leeds (MCA), N.Y.; Fisher.
1898–1952	Henderson, Fletcher: Pace-Handy, N.Y.
1898–	Williams, Clarence: Folkways Recordings.
1899–	Dawson, William: Remuck, N.Y.; Neil Kjos, Park Ridge.
1899–	Ellington, Edward (Duke): Mills Music, N.Y.
	Nickerson, Camille: Handy Bros., N.Y. Leeds, N.Y.
1900–1971	Armstrong, Louis (Satchmo): Melrose Brothers, N.Y.
1901–1967	Work, John Wesley III: Axelrod, Providence; Galaxy.
1904–	Moore, Undine: Gray Music Co.: Witmark, N.Y.
1904–1943	Waller, Thomas (Fats): Schirmer; Santly-Joy, N.Y.
1906–	Basie, William (Count): Decca Recordings.
1909–	Swanson, Howard: Summy-Birchard, Evanston, Illinois.
1910–	Williams, Mary Lou: Verve Recordings.
1911–	Fax, Mark: Contact at Howard University, D.C.
1913–1972	Bond, Margaret: Mercury, N.Y.
1914–1964	Ryder, Noah: J. Fischer, N.Y.
1915–	Kerr, Thomas: Sunny-Birchard, Evanston; E. B. Marks.
1917–	Gillespie, John (Dizzy): Crescendo Recordings.
1917–	Kay, Ulysses: American Composers Alliance; MCA, N.Y.
1920–	Davis, Miles: Columbia Recordings.
1920–1955	Parker, Charlie: Verve Recordings.
1920–	Lewis, John: Atlantic Recordings.
1920–	Monk, Thelonius: Charles Colun, N.Y.
1921–	Taylor, William (Billy): Belwin Mills, N.Y.
1922–	Southall, Mitchell: Handy Brothers; Fischer, N.Y.
1922–	Walker, George: Associated Music; Composers Alliance.
1923–	Kennedy, Joseph: Hema Music Corp., Mt. Vernon, N.Y.
1925–	Harris, Willie: Fan Music Co., Washington, D.C.
1925–	Smith, Hale: Edward B. Marks, N.Y.
1926-1967	Coltrane, John: Impulse Recordings.
1928–	Anderson, Thomas J.: American Composers All., N.Y.
1928–	Cunningham, Arthur: Cunningham Music Co., Nyack.
1930–	Coleman, Ornette: Atlantic Recordings.
1930–	DaCosta, Noel: Edward B. Marks, N.Y.
1930–	Tillis, Frederick: Contact at University/Mass.
1931–	Baker, David: Maher Pub., Chicago; Indiana Univ.
1932–	Perkinson, Coleridge-Taylor: Tosci Music (Frank).
1933–	Jones, Quincy: A & M Recordings.
1933–	Nelson, Oliver: Edward B. Marks, N.Y.

1936–	Moore, Carman: Contact Village Voice News, N.Y.
1937–	Carter, John: Southern Music Publishers, N.Y.
1937–	Wilson, Olly: Contact at Univ. of Cal. at Berkeley.
1940–	Chambers, Stephen: Contact at Brooklyn, N.Y.

Africans

1899–	Amu, Ephraim: University of Ghana, Legon.
1905–	Sowande, Fela: Franco Colombo, N.Y.
1921–	El Dabh, Halim: G. F. Peters Music Corporation, N.Y.
1921–	Nketia, J. Kwabena: University of Ghana, Legon.
1937–	Turkson, Ato: University of Ghana, Legon.

List of Repositories

American Society of African Culture, New York
African Institute, University of Ghana, Legon, Ghana
Detroit Public Library, The Azalia Hackley Room, Michigan
Fisk University, Special Collections Room, Nashville, Tennessee
Hampton Institute, Hampton, Virginia
Howard University, The Moorland Room, Washington, D.C.
Indiana University, Black Music Center, Terre Haute, Indiana
Library of Congress, Music Division, Washington, D.C.
Maryland Historical Society, Baltimore, Maryland
Shomburg Collection, New York City
Talladega College, Alabama
Tuskegee Institute, Alabama
Virginia State College, Black Music Center, Petersburg, Virginia
Yale University, New Haven, Connecticut

INDEX